Purpose and Possibilities

How to Transform Your Life

Elaine J. Brzycki and Henry G. Brzycki

Purpose and Possibilities: How to Transform Your Life

Copyright © 2021 by Henry G. Brzycki and Elaine J. Brzycki

This publication is designed to provide accurate and authoritative information in regard to the subject matter covered. It is sold with the understanding that the author and publisher are not engaged in rendering legal, accounting, psychological, medical or other professional service. If expert assistance is required, the services of a competent professional person should be sought.

Cover concept and design by:
Elaine Brzycki, Henry Brzycki, and Michael Brahosky (MB Designs)

Library of Congress Cataloging-in-Publication Data
Elaine J. Brzycki and Henry G. Brzycki, Purpose and Possibilities: How to Transform Your Life

Includes bibliographical references.
ISBN: 978-0-9887161-9-3 (paper); (Kindle); (PDF)

1. Mental Health and Well-being; 2. Psychological and Physical Well-being; 3. Personal Growth and Development; 4. Self-Help and Improvement

I. Title.
LCCN: 2021905276
Imprint Name: BG Publishing, State College, PA

Printed in the United States of America

Brzyckigroup.com

To each other

About the Book Cover

The cover illustration is based on our pencil sketch of a bright flower, complete with its roots, to metaphorically represent that transformation occurs both internally and externally.

Internal work is represented by the roots, which are mostly unseen, while the beautiful expression of that internal growth into the external world is represented by the flower and leaves.

Continuing the metaphor, the flower does not seek validation from others, but rather has the freedom to be itself and fully express its purpose. Like the flower, you are a unique, wonderful, and essential part of life's unfolding just the way you are.

As a human being, you also have a calling to create a full life for yourself and to make a difference for others. This book helps you to create your fullest life and to make a difference.

Contents

Introduction

A Book About Your Life

Every now and then a book is written that speaks to the consciousness of the time—this is that book for our time. Humanity is seeking deeper meaning in life, a sense of purpose for why life matters, and how to make meaningful changes. This book is for anyone who is seeking a higher purpose in life and wants to see and achieve new possibilities so as to create a happy, healthy, mindful, and flourishing life.

Life for most of us in our contemporary society takes a toll on our emotional, psychological, and physical well-being. We do not have the mental framework, and associated mental capacities, to adequately meet the overwhelming demands of modern life. This inadequacy leaves most people with increasing levels of anxiety and depression; disconnected from their experiences of joy, love, happiness, and inner peace; and lacking a sense of purpose in life with related personal and professional meaning.

How can we impact the troubling ubiquitous human issues that characterize our society, or at least know how to process the daily bombardment? With children being bullied in schools because of ethnic differences or social status; heroin abuse due to post-traumatic stress syndrome; increased adolescent depression, cutting and suicide due to mounting stressors and hopelessness about their futures; increased incidences of sexual assault and alcohol abuse on college campuses; and record levels of being overweight and

1

obese, just to name a few—we think we can agree something is not quite right in our society.

Where do you look to make things better for you, others, and all? It all begins with *you.*

At the outset we want to be totally clear that *this book is about you.* It is about your life. There is no one who knows more about your life than you do—how your life feels, how it is, and how you want it to be. We are asking you to reflect upon how your life is now and how you want it to be. This automatically sets up an important internal and natural dynamic that is good for you.

When reflecting upon your current life you may be aware that something is not quite right, that you do not feel as though you are on the path to seeing and reaching your full and unique potential. Further, you may be so caught up in the past—your family issues, those of your friends, and even the complexities of contemporary life—that you have lost who you are. Being *aware* of this is normal and good.

It is those moments or experiences—when you are feeling you want or desire more in life—that growth and change are possible. However, you must set aside time and space to do the hard work of being totally honest with yourself. We encourage you to do the work on you, for you!

You may be in various stages of growth, but you *are* growing. As the flower on the cover depicts, you are growing deeper within, extending your roots inward, within your soul; and at the same time, you are expressing your self, your full self and unique potential, in the world, making your life and the world a better place for you, others in your life, and for all humankind.

You may be engaging with this book because you are hoping to prevent mental or physical health symptoms or diagnoses. The work you are about to engage in has been used extensively for prevention best practices. Yes, you can prevent suicide, suicide ideation, or self-harm by understanding the importance of prioritizing your own well-being over anything else in your life. Making your emotional well-being a priority and developing your abilities to feel and to experience your life are more important than making others feel better at the expense of your own feelings, as just one example.

You can prevent depression in a number of ways; one pathway is through the physical body and good nutrition. For example, if you are experiencing depression or depressive episodes, you can stop eating too much of certain foods, such as wheat products in breads, pasta, soups, and sauces. Wheat interacts with your blood in a similar manner as alcohol and is turned into sugars rapidly for an immediate feelgood sensation, then a crash of blood sugars. Further, the lectins in wheat interact with your digestive tract in such a manner as to slow its rate of flow. The health risks and implications of this potential digestive issue are profound and wide.

There are also emotional consequences, such as feeling bad about yourself that you feel so sluggish, as well as negative self-talk that you are not addressing your weight or health issues. This negative self-talk can spiral downward and put you into a depressive state.

Yet many people would not even consider the possibility of exploring nutritional preventive measures because it would question habits developed over years or generations. We encourage you to explore the numerous types of nutritional programs that best fit your body and blood type. Opening yourself up to possibilities requires a willingness to look for and consider new approaches that may be beyond your current understanding.

"Possibilities" are potential states of being that take you beyond your current thinking to new perspectives heretofore unavailable to you. Specifically, new psychological or cognitive possibilities are always available to you, new pathways to create a new you and new life. This is often exciting and transforms your mindset from resignation to a sense of possibilities, along with concomitant positive emotions and new life circumstances; it is like seeing current circumstances through a new lens. What we are discussing is the psychology of well-being and the integrated relationship between mind and body—your mind-body connection.

You may also be in need of self-healing due to a childhood or young adulthood trauma. Traumas separate yourself from your life, from fully experiencing your life. This is clinically known as "dissociation," where your ability to feel in daily life is muted, dampened, or numbed. Recall the popular classic rock band Pink Floyd song lyric, "We have become comfortably numb." The methods in this book can help you heal or repair your emotional separation due to trauma.

Remember that trauma, sadness, loss, and grief are a part of life, and if you have experienced these things, you are just like every other human being in the world. However, if you are *currently* experiencing psychological or physical trauma or any kind of abuse, seek professional assistance right away, or reach out to a trusted individual who can refer you to professional assistance. Putting your well-being first and foremost means getting out of harm's way as soon as you can.

You may also want to use this book for self-growth: to self-reflect, learn more about who you are and why you are the way you are, and inquire into your unique destiny and purpose in life and what possibilities are available to you that you have not been aware of or seen.

From time to time when breakdowns occur on the path of our lives, we need to take some time for ourselves in order to put into the most effective context or perspective possible the issues and concerns that are showing up as obstacles, limitations, or restrictions. These issues and concerns usually present themselves during significant life transitions; they can dramatically impact our ability to see and achieve what is possible for ourselves and our relationships, families, children, professional life, organizations, and community. Family and societal constraints—in the form, most often, of personally formed or shaped beliefs—are the most dominant.

One example of how both conscious and unconscious beliefs can influence your thinking about yourself and your life is from a family whose members were suffering from heart disease and obesity; the mother and two children were all diagnosed as obese. When interviewed about how they think and feel about their current unhealthy condition, they were aware that they were not healthy and that obesity contributes to numerous additional health problems, noting the eldest son had developed a heart condition. When asked about his deteriorating condition, he stated that obesity and heart problems run in his family and that his father died from heart disease, as did his grandfather, and most likely he would too. He was matter-of-fact in his description and was clear of his potential direction with predictable outcome. While in rare instances there are some people with irreversible congenital heart conditions, medical science tells us the overwhelming majority of heart issues are behavior based, and therefore, with a change of mindset and new behaviors, they are preventable.

Yet when asked if he wanted guidance on how to change his current situation and learn how to eat, exercise, and make fundamental personal changes, he was resigned to his most likely future and declined. Even the invitation to learn how to cook healthier foods was declined. "Why?" you may ask.

Clearly, he was locked into his beliefs about health and family; and somehow these beliefs learned in his family culture were a more powerful and dominant force guiding his thinking and feelings about his own self, his health, and life trajectories. In fact, you could state that adhering to these beliefs were more important than changing them. He most likely felt the only heart-felt connection with family members when commiserating about common health issues.

Why don't people of any age—adolescents, young adults, or adults—more often take self-responsibility and self-initiative to tap into their inner drive to create a better self and a better world? Most often it is because they are trapped in their own minds, with unexamined beliefs and assumptions about who they are "supposed to be." This false self is learned through family systems that permit only certain values, customs, and behaviors that are deemed acceptable, while emotions deemed somehow unacceptable are suppressed by the family culture.

In the case of our unhealthy family, the difficulties and sadness about family members' health became a way of feeling close to each other and the family as a whole, and each took on the identity of the family as their own. In short, they found comfort. A false self is shaped; each individual did not know who they were separate from the family, nor how they each felt about their physical condition. No one feels good when they are obese or suffering from a heart condition. You do not have the energy to accomplish simple daily tasks and goals, let alone dream of a life that demands more energy from you in order to achieve.

This false self is also learned through our contemporary culture with its own set of limited acceptable values, customs, behaviors, and emotions. And, as you can readily determine, these forces are extremely powerful, omnipresent, ubiquitous, and destructive. These forces can be destructive to the full expression of a person's own sense of self and of their own inner sense of a destiny in life, and even to basic human instincts and emotions that serve as a source of inner motivation to grow and change and make a unique contribution to the greater good.

Another false self can be generated by your own ego. The ego is reactivated when a situation is presented that evokes emotions such as fear, shame, anxiety, anger, or the need to dominate others. When you are confronted in such a manner that you find yourself defending or acting out in fear or anger toward another, your ego is being asked by your inner self to redesign the identity that has been shaped around it. Your identity is made up of a basket or collection of beliefs learned through life experiences.

When you realize it costs you more to hold onto your ego's identity, instead of redesigning your inner self's identity—toward a new set of beliefs more suited to your current and future life, and vision of who you want to become—you are left with an inner peace, a calm. You no longer have to defend your old self or old ego or outdated identity. This process is constantly occurring, and therefore you are changing perpetually, literally every second, with every breath, with every new experience.

How to change and grow

You want to change and grow! This is fundamental to who you are; you cannot help this natural force that resides deep within you. Some call this undeniable force your spirit or drive to manifest your own sense of your destiny. It is in your self-interest to change—you benefit! If you are constantly changing anyway, you may as well take charge of the processes of change and go in the direction you want.

Changes can happen cognitively, emotionally, physically, or all of these holistically—mind, body, soul. When one part of you changes, it is like a mobile; all parts are impacted to varying degrees.

Helping people to define and then change themselves to become the person they want to become and are meant to be is possible, and there are methods that have been used for 40 years that transform lives. The first step in the change process is to ask questions that reveal your deep-seated dreams and highest vision for yourself, your relationships, and your community or society more broadly. Questions— such as "What are my highest hopes and dreams for my life?"—can be asked through every one of your day-to-day experiences, during personal reflection time, and in your family, school-based settings, workplace, and community.

We have been impressed with the degree to which people of all ages who engage in these questions make positive changes in the direction of their own vision of success. We have worked with people of all ages who are ready to actively engage in these questions about the inner self. Because of its universality, this inquiry is appropriate for any stage in life, whether that stage brings a focus on action and achievement or contemplation and completion.

Families, schools, and other organizations typically do not place a high priority or importance upon freeing you up to discover your unique purpose and to realize new possibilities. They, unfortunately, are more concerned about instilling beliefs to ensure that you fit in, or buy into the prevailing system of beliefs. It is ultimately up to you to rise above any and all family dynamics or what you learned in school, and create *you*. This does not mean that you completely reject any and all of your family beliefs, or those of your local community, only that you come to know that you are separate and distinct, and not embedded in these beliefs. You can choose to embrace them to become larger than your circumstances, a bigger person in terms of your sense of higher purpose in your life.

We have provided leadership to individuals, families, K-16 schools, and other organizations, where the overarching framework for social emotional learning, student success, and student well-being is grounded in the psychology of well-being, putting well-being first to empower resilience and success across the lifespan. This is why we have written this book—to place the power of a happy, healthy, flourishing life directly in the hands of people. This eliminates the need to rely upon often-times absent support services offered in families, schools, therapists' offices, or other institutions. Even when those services are necessary, available, and workable, you are better served when *you* take the responsibility for choosing them and envision what you want to accomplish by using the service.

We want to place the methods or best practices in your hands to do what is best for you.

Research demonstrates that people are not emerging from their family upbringing nor educational system with the mental framework and associated mental capacities to adequately meet the overwhelming demands of modern life. The issue of mental health and well-being is becoming more and more acute as life in modern society becomes more and more complex. People have expanded needs and more mental and physical challenges and illnesses. Our society is not adequately addressing or measuring these needs and challenges. As a result, we are seeing dire and overwhelming statistics on bullying, hate crimes, trauma, anxiety, depression, sexual assault, substance abuse, suicide, behavior-based physical illnesses, and more.

People in our society are not well. We are in the middle of a well-being crisis. We have much work to do in the world to communicate our ideas on how to help humanity through these times.

The role of emotions

Emotions are important because they motivate us to grow and develop and make a difference in the world—the real world. Without emotions and motivated reasoning, change is not possible. When you know what you want, and you are passionate about it for whatever reason, "structural tension" is created. Structural tension is a clinical term to describe the energy created when an individual concurrently envisions a desired future state, while being completely aware of the limitations of present or current reality. The difference between the desired future state and current reality creates a tension that seeks resolution toward one or the other. (We further describe this tension and the related first axiom of structural dynamics in Chapter 7.)

In any relationship, such as the one between the current self and the new self you want to create, it is critical to establish this structural tension in order to empower positive change. When this tension is created, emotional thought drives the change process. It is your responsibility to guide positive changes and utilize methods so you can learn how to do this for yourself. Passion is a powerful emotion that can be understood and should be encouraged to the benefit of every person. Often, the dynamic that compels you to want to change is your soul speaking to you that you are not living the life you are meant to live—your higher calling in life. It is important to listen to what your soul is saying, to put words and feelings to what you are hearing.

This dynamic is powerful because you are really powerful. Using this dynamic, you can open up a new possibility that heretofore was unavailable to you. It is our hope that while reading this book, you will discover your own personal pathway to a happy, healthy, flourishing life filled with new possibilities in every aspect of your life.

People often change the entire course of their lives as they fully experience and learn how to create what they want to create using the methods and discussions in this book.

You can use this book to move from responding or reacting to life as it seems to be, to directly creating the experiences and quality of life you want. It could be a commitment to reaching for that which is *highest* in yourself. You are the artist in and of your life, "and all of the colors I am inside have not been invented yet" (Shel Silverstein). You are that flower in the field, or in the garden, that is wanting to show your inner beauty to the world, because you can do no other. Your spirit and soul are more powerful than your mind and body. You can listen to your soul's message and honor it; this is always what humans want.

"Happiness makes up in height for what it lacks in length" (Robert Frost). As you shift your emotions from numb (negative) to enlivened (positive), they build a well to draw upon, accumulate over time, and put you on a trajectory of growth by broadening your awareness of the possible and building your capabilities to flourish in life. When you are in touch with your higher purpose, you are naturally happy, kind, giving, loving.

The wealth of benefits of positive emotions is well documented. They improve physical health. They foster trust and compassion. They buffer against depressive symptoms and help people recover from stress. They can even undo the undesirable effects of negative emotions. With frequent experience and expression of positive emotions comes resilience and resourcefulness. Moreover, positive emotions foster better social connectedness.

By choosing to read this book you have made a choice about your life. You have chosen well-being, satisfaction, future possibilities, and personal growth toward your unique potential. We hope you will see the power of that choice.

It is during your reading that you will experience that you are powerful—you will learn powerful methods to transform yourself and your life. The methods in this book have been utilized by professional counselors, advisors, psychologists, teachers, researchers, parents, students, and medical professionals to see and achieve new possibilities. Because these impactful methods focus on *you* and *your* purpose, they are always relevant to your current experience.

Bottom line, the entire focus of this book—with its methods, discussions, and reflections—is intended to shift your view of yourself and the world to place yourself at the center of your paradigm of reality—like looking through a new lens to envision and create a happy, healthy, and flourishing life.

Your purpose as your North Star

A sense of purpose is an important attribute that can be learned. Studies find that pursuing one's purpose is associated with psychological well-being. Much like the North Star glows as a constant guide in the sky, your purpose guides your life.

Individuals with a sense of purpose report they are happier, more satisfied with their lives, and more hopeful about the future. Knowing your purpose is also associated with physical health, including lower stress hormone levels, improved cardiovascular and metabolic markers, reduced pain, a regression in some cancers, and longevity.

Living on purpose feels alive, clear, and authentic, and those who are purposeful may experience "flow," a state of total absorption in which time seems to disappear and a person can feel content and fulfilled. Our research and work show people transform their quality of life when they identify a higher purpose that is driving their thoughts, feelings, and actions.

Exploring a sense of purpose can awaken awareness of one's unique interests, strengths, and values and provide a focus for specific projects, academic choices, careers, and loving relationships. On a larger scale, purpose can inform a lifetime of relationships, community involvement, citizenship, and spirituality.

Learning about purpose is not meant to intimidate you with fears you may never find your "perfect path," but rather to provide pathways through adversity to a higher calling. We encourage you to consider your inner and spiritual calling to contribute to the human condition in a way that is unique to your life experiences and views of the greater good.

How this book is organized

This book is organized in 10 sequential chapters, each building upon the previous one. The chapters contain discussions and self-reflections intended to help you experience new possibilities in the way you see yourself and the world, and in your abilities to have an impact. Within each discussion you will have access to one of our evidence-based methods for helping you to live the life you want and are meant to live. It is very important you utilize these methods by reflecting upon the attributes presented and draw each attribute back to yourself.

This book and work engage you in learning about your whole self, mind-body-soul. When you engage in the methods, you will be learning how to access new experiences of who you are, have been, and want to become. In our view learning is the pathway to your transformation. We have pioneered these methods that produce mental health and well-being outcomes, and now you have access to this body of work.

We have organized this book in such a way as to give you access to your whole self and transformation from a prior self to a new self—a more evolved and enlightened self. It is our intent to provide the learning resources that reveal and empower what is going on inside of you, at your subconscious and intuitive levels of your consciousness.

There are one or two Reflections per chapter, for a total of 15 Reflections throughout the book. Reflections are activities that require you to reflect, observe, and create. Your self-assessments from the Reflections are meant to be brought into your daily life as part of your mindful, moment-to-moment awareness.

Before beginning a Reflection, first breathe deeply for a few minutes and relax your entire body. To record your thoughts and emotions, you may wish to purchase a separate notebook so you are not constrained by the number of pages we provide in this book. Though you may also choose to record your thoughts on an electronic device, we recommend using a pen, pencil, marker, or paintbrush directly in this book, on separate pieces of paper, or in a notebook to tap into your full consciousness.

When you write, don't edit yourself. Let your writing flow openly using individual words, phrases, or sentences. Realize the self-assessments you will be conducting are not final answers, but rather your own mindful observations at this moment in time to help yourself grow and explore new possibilities. Do your best to observe yourself in your own life with *curiosity* and *not* judgement.

We suggest that you start at the beginning, with Chapter 1, in which we present the eight dimensions of well-being or wellness. It is essential to prioritize well-being in your life if you want to see and achieve your unique potentials. Additionally, you will feel something occurring at the subconscious level; this is your integrity speaking to your conscious mind that you want more, a vision, in each of the well-being dimensions.

As you move on to Chapter 2 you will be challenged to reflect upon the quotations presented in context with what is coming up for you in terms of new emotions, experiences, and thoughts. In a moment of insight and honesty you may see you have developed a "false self" in order to fit into and receive conditional love from your family. Or you may realize you have closed off your heart and do not love to your fullest abilities, which is at your core self. This is the value in providing yourself with the space to reflect.

In Chapter 3 you come to a more complex and sophisticated way to your own self-knowledge with a framework that helps you understand. You will come to know that self-awareness is much more than self-esteem or emotional intelligence. For example, you may have the insight that daily life for you has lost its meaning, and that you have elevated looking good to others to a higher level of importance and energy exerted in your life. This is another opportunity to create a new vision or picture of your future self.

In Chapter 4, you will have the opportunity to reflect on how to connect your whole self to well-being factors and to honestly assess and determine opportunities to grow and change personally and professionally.

Chapter 5 takes you to a deeper level of understanding about what has kept you from seeing possibilities in your life and to creating new experiences that are more along the lines of what you want, what you can envision. This will undoubtedly be an emotional experience for you, so please prepare yourself and know these emotions are healthy for you to feel and complete—it is to your advantage.

As in all of the Reflections in each chapter, take as much time as you need; please do not hurry through the details or procedures within each, nor rush the time required to thoroughly work through or process the thoughts and emotions that may emerge. Further, take each Reflection out into your life, into the real world, beyond the intimate and private space you are using to read and go through each Reflection. In this way you will be gaining mastery over your life and how to actively create positive changes that you want.

In Chapter 6 you will have the opportunity to do your own mindfulness exercise, through a self-guided meditation. This is actually such a fun and rewarding and deeply satisfying meditation. Each time you visit this mindful place, keep in mind all of the self attributes learned thus far, and note your growth in accessing your source of power, your inner self.

You will reach a peak or a high point to your experiences in Chapters 7 and 8 through completing The Success Predictor. You will put together your "DNA of consciousness," the various levels of your self, and the future you can imagine and thus create. The DNA of consciousness works much like the molecular structure containing the genetic code guiding your cells what proteins to make. When you complete The Success Predictor, you will have the structure of your consciousness that provides guidance for your thoughts, feelings, and actions.

You will align your highest calling and purpose in life, with what you see is possible for you and humanity, with direct pathways to implement these in your life and in the world. This is hard, deep work and worth every effort. You will see and experience a whole new you either immediately or throughout The Success Predictor process—truly exciting!

Chapter 9 is your opportunity to put together your team members upon whom you can rely to support the new you, your transformed self, and the future you are creating. Support is important—you cannot do this life alone.

Chapters 10 is about learning just how great you are, through acknowledging even the most minute results or accomplishments throughout your daily life. This is also your opportunity to acknowledge others in your life for what they have done for you thus far; it is truly powerful to experience the depth of joy and happiness and love with those who have meant so much to you.

Take all of the time you need to do the most important work of your life! Enjoy the journey.

Chapter 1

Creating a Well-Being Centered Life

Living a successful and satisfying life requires well-being, therefore we need to understand what well-being is. The figure in the following Reflection depicts a holistic understanding of the eight dimensions that make up "wellness" (Brzycki and Brzycki, 2016). Note that we use well-being and wellness interchangeably.

~ REFLECTION ~
Eight dimensions of your well-being

You may not have previously thought about your own well-being or each of the eight dimensions—emotional, environmental, physical, occupational, spiritual, social, financial—and how you are doing in each. Take a moment to read each dimension and do a self-assessment by ranking them from your healthiest to your least healthy or, alternately, according to how much you pay attention to them in your daily life. You may have a realization that you have neglected one or more and therefore feel badly about how this happened. In this case, you are having a realization that your well-being is complicated, multi-dimensional, and could be something to prioritize in your life as you create a vision of your future. By simply noticing your awareness of the dimensions, you have used them to grow and change and develop—congratulations!

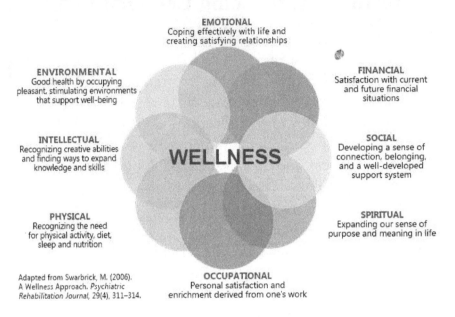

EMOTIONAL
Coping effectively with life and creating satisfying relationships

ENVIRONMENTAL
Good health by occupying pleasant, stimulating environments that support well-being

FINANCIAL
Satisfaction with current and future financial situations

INTELLECTUAL
Recognizing creative abilities and finding ways to expand knowledge and skills

WELLNESS

SOCIAL
Developing a sense of connection, belonging, and a well-developed support system

PHYSICAL
Recognizing the need for physical activity, diet, sleep and nutrition

SPIRITUAL
Expanding our sense of purpose and meaning in life

Adapted from Swarbrick, M. (2006). A Wellness Approach. *Psychiatric Rehabilitation Journal*, 29(4), 311–314.

OCCUPATIONAL
Personal satisfaction and enrichment derived from one's work

Rank the dimensions from your healthiest to your least healthy or, if you prefer, according to how much you pay attention to them in your daily life. What possibilities emerge if you were to change the ranking order in your life?

1.
2.
3.
4.
5.
6.
7.
8.

Well-being is not simply the absence of mental or physical illness. Rather, it is the more positive connotation of how well your life is going. Well-being encompasses emotional health, vitality and satisfaction; life direction; ability to make a difference; the quality of one's relationships; and living a good life (Brown and LaJambe, 2016).

We also want to make it clear that people with health ailments or obstacles, whether congenital, acute or chronic, can have well-being if they take care of themselves and balance the other dimensions of wellness.

We cannot think of wellness in one single dimension, meaning each of the eight dimensions of wellness overlap into a whole or holistic model. For example, one of the dimensions of wellness in the figure is "occupational," the satisfaction or sense of accomplishment from a career. This dimension interacts with "intellectual, financial, social, emotional," and most likely all eight dimensions to varying degrees.

Wellness is actually a broader concept that includes understanding purpose and meaning in life or the "spiritual" dimension, developing a sense of belonging, taking care of physical needs, understanding intellectual strengths and unique capabilities, understanding financial management and support for lifestyle choices, and developing the ability to feel a full range of emotions, including resentments and regrets, anger and sadness, and happiness and joy.

~ REFLECTION ~
Your first opportunity to experience unconscious and internal energy changes

Before beginning this Reflection, please close your eyes, breathe deeply, and relax your entire body. When you are ready, open your eyes and answer the following three questions:

1. Describe what you would like to accomplish out of reading and experiencing this book. Please be certain to describe what you want in all aspects of your life—psychological, emotional, and physical well-being, self-understanding, relationships, direction in life, personal development, career aspirations, motivations to change, and spiritual calling, among others. Be as precise and clear as possible. (As a reminder, you may wish to write your responses in a separate notebook so you are not constrained by the number of pages we provide).

2. Please describe your present or current situation including all of your needs for well-being, self-understanding, and developmental needs, to the best of your ability. Be certain to include detailed descriptions regarding your spiritual, physical, emotional, and psychological conditions and symptoms.

3. What have been the most significant experiences in your life thus far? Why were they so meaningful to you?

Additional space …

Chapter 2

Reflecting on Personal Meaning

Whenever you self-reflect, observe what is coming up for you in terms of new emotions, thoughts, physical sensations, and experiences. Give yourself the time and space to reflect and for a wide range of emotions and thoughts to arise.

~ REFLECTION ~
Quotes that evoke meaning for you

Inspiring and thought-provoking words from writers, leaders, psychologists, philosophers, and historical figures can help provide a wider range of possibilities. We have included a number of quotes that have inspired or challenged us. Read the quotes and then answer the questions that follow them.

We ask ourselves, "Who am I to be brilliant, gorgeous, talented, and fabulous?"
Actually, who are you not to be?
— Marianne Williamson

You see things; and you say, "Why?"
But I dream things that never were; and I say, "Why not?"
— George Bernard Shaw

There is always light, if only we're brave enough to see it.
If only we're brave enough to be it.
— Amanda Gorman

Sometimes we try to make our feelings disappear because we are afraid of them. To acknowledge how we really feel would demand a decision— action or change—on our part ... We would become aware of what we're thinking, what we want, and what we need to do.
— Melody Beattie

The core self contains an essential humanity whose nature is peace and whose expression is thought and whose action is unconditional love. When we identify with that inner core, respecting and honoring it in others as well as ourselves, we experience healing in every area of our lives.
— Joan Borysenko

I believe that modernity has persistently and systematically misunderstood women—their motives, their moral commitments, the course of their psychological growth, and their special view of what is important in life.
— Carol Gilligan

It is not true that people stop pursuing dreams because they grow old, they grow old because they stop pursuing dreams.
— Gabriel García Márquez

In order to believe she is loved, the child behaves the way she thinks she is <u>supposed</u> to. This false self develops over the years and is reinforced by the family system's needs, and by culture."
— John Bradshaw

Every act of creation begins with an act of destruction.
— Picasso

Since the artist cares in a peculiar way for the phase of experience in which union is achieved, he does not shun moments of resistance and tension. He rather cultivates them, not for their own sake but because of their potentialities, bringing to living consciousness an experience that is unified and total.
— John Dewey, *Art as Experience*

The privilege of a lifetime is being who you are.
— Joseph Campbell

I pray to the God within me that He will give me the strength to ask Him the right questions.
— Elie Wiesel

Just as man cannot live without dreams, he cannot live without hope. If dreams reflect the past, hope summons the future.
— Elie Wiesel

Welcome, O life! I go to encounter for the millionth time the reality of experience and to forge in the smithy of my soul the uncreated conscience of my race.
— James Joyce, *A Portrait of the Artist as a Young Man*

Taking into consideration your responses from the previous chapter about your hopes and dreams, which of the previous quotes have personal meaning for you? Why?

Do you have any favorite quotes that hold personal meaning to you? Write them down and reflect on why they are meaningful to you. These can be old favorites, newly discovered ones, or the words of someone you know and admire.

Additional space ...

Chapter 3

Knowing Your Self as the Source of All Possibilities: The Integrated Self

We have established that living a successful and satisfying life requires self-knowledge, so it is time to dive deeper into understanding the self as the source of possibilities.

The "self" may be defined as the essential or particular qualities that distinguish one person from another, such as personality traits or talents. However, it can be even more useful in personal development, self-improvement, teaching, learning, and counseling to think of the self as a holistic system with three major components: the body, the mind, and the soul.

In the context of psychology, the mind is "an organic system reaching all parts of the body and serving to adjust the total organism to the demands of the environment" (Friend & Guralnik, 1953). When we talk about the mind, we are generally talking about processes such as cognition and meta-cognition, conscious thought, and emotions.

The root of the word psychology, "psyc," comes from the Greek word psyche, which means soul. It is helpful to consider the soul as those aspects of the self often beyond words, yet essential to our being. When we talk about soul, we are referring to the inner self and vital processes such as hope, character, integrity, and spirituality, as well as sometimes unrecognized emotions that guide the conscious mind toward a higher purpose. All these aspects of the person unite as the self.

Learning about the self is really the same when reading, engaging in daily activities, taking classes in traditional classroom educational settings, growing professionally, and participating in therapeutic counseling, in that the pathway to learning is through psychological processes that are personally meaningful. In all contexts or environments, the goal is similar: to lay the groundwork for a flourishing life.

The self is important to know and understand because it mediates the inner life with the outer life to determine our realities and shape a positive life course.

Reading this chapter, you will see the connection between the whole self, the components that make up the self, and how new possibilities are created. This is an exciting dynamic to experience.

We developed the Integrated Self Model (the "iSelf"), a holistic model with a multidimensional understanding of 30 component parts—called "self attributes"—that make up the self as depicted in the following diagram (Brzycki and Brzycki, 2009, 2016, 2019). When one self attribute changes, as in a mobile, all attributes are impacted to varying degrees. Also, your self attributes are shaped by and, in turn, shape external and cultural experiences.

The Integrated Self™ Model

Mind-Body-Soul

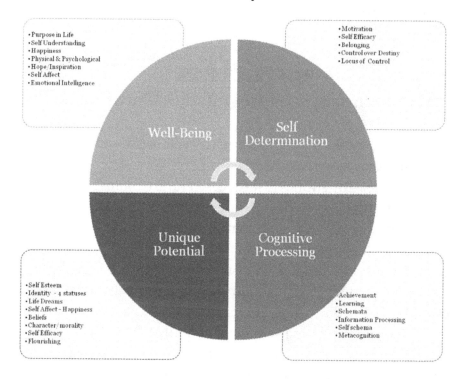

- Purpose in Life
- Self Understanding
- Happiness
- Physical & Psychological
- Hope/Inspiration
- Self Affect
- Emotional Intelligence

- Motivation
- Self Efficacy
- Belonging
- Control over Destiny
- Locus of Control

Well-Being

Self Determination

Unique Potential

Cognitive Processing

- Self Esteem
- Identity - 4 statuses
- Life Dreams
- Self Affect - Happiness
- Beliefs
- Character/morality
- Self Efficacy
- Flourishing

- Achievement
- Learning
- Schemata
- Information Processing
- Self schema
- Metacognition

External and Cultural Experiences

This model incorporates concepts from educational psychology (which is the science of learning), developmental psychology (which studies the self as the sum of dynamic component parts), and positive psychology (which studies ways people can flourish in their lives).

Interacting with the model's self attributes heightens self-knowledge exponentially, which helps you grow and expands your ability to see and achieve your potential. When explored, the self attributes open up a world of possibilities for a purposeful, fulfilling, and happy life. We hope these attributes are as helpful, enlightening, and inspiring as we found them to be in our own lives. Continue with this section in the spirit of discovery.

~ REFLECTION ~
Experiencing the Integrated Self attributes

Read each of the following self attributes. Some attributes may sound similar to others, so please take the time to notice any subtle differences. The attributes are listed in no particular order to encourage curiosity and understanding that each attribute interacts with all of the others.

First, rate yourself on your strength in each attribute from one to five. You may alternately choose to rate your awareness of the attribute in your life.

Now review the list again to identify at least three (3) attributes for which you gave yourself a higher rating relative to the others. Acknowledge yourself for being aware of these attributes, and then write in the space beneath each of your selected attributes some of the ways you have drawn upon or experienced them in your life and how you can continue to access them as strengths.

Now select at least one (1) attribute you have more rarely or never experienced before. In the space beneath the attribute, answer these questions: "What would it look like in your life if you were more often aware of this attribute?" and "How can this attribute open new possibilities to more fully express yourself in day-to-day life?"

Self-Concept

Self-concept is how you view yourself; your frame made up of important references. Self-image and self-perception are synonymous terms. Important references can be your interests and activities. These interests are usually grouped or categorized (e.g., academic and nonacademic, peer group or friends, intellectual and nonintellectual, physical and nonphysical, athletic and nonathletic, artistic and non-artistic, among others).

Self-concept most often develops through becoming aware of innate strengths and developing qualities and characteristics and the quality of the experience of performance when exercising these. It develops through a process of attempting to express an innate desire or interest combined with the messages received through the experience. An individual's innate cognitive strengths are commonly organized along the lines of Howard Gardner's Theory of Multiple Intelligences (1983), which includes strengths defined as interpersonal and intrapersonal, naturalistic and spiritual, logical and linguistic, kinesthetic and spatial, and musical and artistic.

Rating: 1 2 3 4 5

Reflections:

Self-Esteem

Self-esteem refers to the values you place upon those strengths, characteristics, and activities that make up your self-concept—such as feeling good or bad about your abilities in math, sports, music, leadership, empathy, or feeling deeply, as examples. Numerous scholars and researchers have found a direct correlation between self-esteem and performance.

The following quote underscores the important connection between negative self-esteem and therefore negative self-system constructs and well-being outcomes: "a child who experiences attachment figures as rejecting or emotionally unavailable and non-supportive will construct a working model of the self as unlovable, incompetent, and generally unworthy" (Harter, 1999).

Individuals with diminished self-esteem can rebuild it and construct a new model of the self by noticing false assumptions and identifying previously unacknowledged strengths.

Rating: 1 2 3 4 5
Reflections:

Self-Efficacy

Self-efficacy is your belief about your potentials and about your capacity to grow and learn to become the person you want to become. It is the belief you can accomplish a goal. The first source of efficacy is mastery experiences, which are our direct experiences of success or failure. Successes raise our efficacy beliefs, and failures lower our efficacy beliefs.

The second source of efficacy is physiological and emotional arousal, which impacts efficacy beliefs depending on whether we are anxious or worried (low efficacy) or excited or happy (high efficacy).

The third is vicarious experience, which ties our efficacy beliefs to someone who models accomplishments and the degree to which we identify with the model. When the model performs well, our efficacy increases, but when the model performs poorly, our efficacy expectations decrease.

The fourth, social persuasion, uses the power of performance feedback to boost efficacy expectations, but efficacy will only be enhanced if the persuader is credible, trustworthy, and an expert.

You can heighten self-efficacy by redefining success or failure from a broader perspective or by reframing limiting assumptions you may have made about your emotional responses.

Rating: 1 2 3 4 5
Reflections:

Self-Understanding

Self-understanding is the conscious knowing that you are a separate self from the external world—your circumstances, family, peers, social media, other media and technology, culture, and society. It is the knowing you have a separate way of feeling, experiencing events, and interpreting the world and a personal understanding of your uniqueness vis-à-vis others.

Self-understanding is sometimes used in other contexts synonymously with self-knowledge; however, in this book, there is a distinction. Self-knowledge is the sum or holistic view of your self in all of its component parts as described in the Integrated Self Model. Self-understanding is one component part or attribute, important in that it allows you to be separate from others and from your circumstances or even past beliefs and assumptions.

This attribute is important in that often we do not have healthy boundaries between ourselves and others, or between ourselves and our control over substances such as unhealthy foods, drugs, and alcohol. Expressions of self-understanding include higher and higher levels of consciousness, awareness that there are higher states and that they contribute to enlightened views. Adolescents and young adults who possess self-understanding grow up to be more accomplished in the domain of school and later in life as healthier adults.

Rating: 1 2 3 4 5
Reflections:

Identity

Identity is the set of behavioral or personal traits by which you are recognizable to yourself and others. Identity refers to your distinct personality, including such traits as having character, morality, and integrity. People often mistakenly think identity is unchanging, however, we form and reform our identities over the course of a lifetime and at different and distinct stages of development.

Identity can be experienced as a sense of psychosocial well-being or a feeling of being at home in one's body, a sense of "knowing where one is going," and an inner assuredness of anticipated recognition from those who count. Such a sense of identity, however, is never gained nor maintained once and for all. Like a "good conscience," it is constantly lost and regained. Identity is a belief or set of beliefs about who you are or think you are (Erikson, 1980).

Developmental psychology describes four identity statuses in which people explore options and commit to pursuing an action; explore options but delay any commitments; do not explore options, but commit based on what others tell them to do; or neither explore nor commit (Marcia, 1991, 2002).

Character is formed or shaped through life experiences that both create and inform each of the self attributes. Character is achieved when there is an alignment—or integrity—among your purpose, dreams, and commitments, and when your approaches to achieving these are aligned with the results that show up in your day-to-day reality.

At any stage in life, it is important to accept your life and reflect positively upon how your identity has changed and will change in the future. Achieving a sense of integrity means fully accepting yourself—the good and the not so good. Accepting responsibility for your life circumstances—and being able to correct mistakes from the past to reorient your life toward your moral compass—are essential. The inability to do this results in a feeling of despair. In today's world, too many of us feel despair, and we lack integrity because we do not know ourselves.

Rating: 1 2 3 4 5

Reflections:

Locus of Control

Locus of control refers to your belief system regarding the causes of experiences and the factors to which you attribute success or failure. There is a critical distinction between internal and external locus of control in assessing beliefs about who has influence over one's life course.

A healthy internal locus of control suggests that an individual attributes success to their own efforts and abilities. A person who expects to succeed will be more internally motivated and more likely to want to learn, take full responsibility for the circumstances in their life, and know they can change them to manifest their own destiny in life.

External locus of control suggests that an individual attributes success to luck or fate or to circumstances outside of their self and control. People with external locus of control are more likely to experience anxiety, resignation, depression, and withdrawal from fully experiencing life—to be a victim of their circumstances.

Rating: 1 2 3 4 5

Reflections:

Self-Affect

Self-affect refers to a personal feeling or emotion that is sometimes difficult to use language to describe because it is an experience. It involves multiple sensations to varying degrees.

Without affect, your feelings have no intensity, and without "feeling your feelings," your ability to think and make rational decisions is reduced. In short, self-affect is the ability to feel and to know you are feeling emotions.

Rating: 1 2 3 4 5

Reflections:

Life Purpose and Spirituality

Life purpose is the reason you are here, for your existence (raison d'être), and it describes or includes your basic nature or being: the essence of a human being, the totality of all things that exist, the qualities that constitute existence or essence, and your basic nature. It includes your mission in life as an avenue or pathway to manifest your purpose—an inner calling to pursue an activity or perform a service, a vocation, the area of life where you will manifest your purpose. This calling can be spiritual in nature and involves a connection with a higher power, an uplifting and transcending force, or feeling of need: to feel the calling to contribute to the human condition in some way, unique to you and your life experiences and views of a better world or greater good.

It is what we commit our lives to, bigger than ourselves, using our unique talents, values, and vision in the service of creating a better world. It is part of the underlying motivation and driving force that guides our actions and brings us fulfillment.

Our purpose is bigger than we are; it is a lifelong process that we can continuously discover and improve upon, and it compels us to make a difference in our lives, the lives of others, and the condition of the world.

Rating: 1 2 3 4 5

Reflections:

Life Meaning

People of all ages and backgrounds are seeking meaningful experiences and a meaningful life. This involves being able to process the vast amounts of information that you take in constantly and then create meaning, a deeper understanding, connecting with the attributes of the self.

This is the process of interpreting information as relevant to some aspect of yourself or your life, special to you and the way you interpret life events. You are taking information and consciously placing meaning on it.

Rating: 1 2 3 4 5

Reflections:

Intrinsic Motivation

Intrinsic motivation refers to your inner drive to achieve or reach a desired state. This inner drive may come from instinct, a deep subconscious desire, or a conscious want, and it is usually juxtaposed with extrinsic motivation, which refers to the external forces that move you to act. Learning adds to and changes our internal motivations to manifest that which we desire for our best self-interest.

When you learn you have a new belief about the importance of relationships and you choose to define yourself by this belief, then you are internally motivated to develop meaningful relationships that reinforce your belief system. People who are intrinsically motivated pursue an activity to gain skills they deem important, make ethical and moral choices, or experience pleasure.

Rating: 1 2 3 4 5

Reflections:

Happiness

Happiness is an emotion of elation, of joy, of feeling all is well. An experience interpreted as a state of being happy, it is a conscious thought. The term subjective happiness is often used because there is no absolute state; it is an interpretation of an experience that makes you happy. While feelings of elation can be temporarily created in our brain with mood-altering drugs or other substances, lasting happiness requires more proactive awareness and decision-making. It is often said happiness is a choice.

The experience reflects a deeper want has been realized. This deeper want may be a conscious or intuitive desire. Satisfaction is an example of a feeling of happiness—evidence that a want or desire or intended result has been realized or manifest. Happiness occurs when the resulting circumstances in your life match your dreams, commitments, and goals for your life, after taking action or implementing a strategy to produce results.

People thrive on having goals, and there are always more goals to set for the future; happiness requires finding a dynamic equilibrium between your wants and the evidence that these wants will be or have been achieved.

Rating: 1 2 3 4 5
Reflections:

Inspiration, Hope, and Dreams

Inspiration, hope, and dreams all involve a vision of a future state, including all circumstances and emotions: what you can see that you want in your mind's eye. You are inspired to dream, to spark the insight or seed of a desired future state through inspiration either from another person or within your inner life or life experience; you hope that you can manifest that dream. It is what you see in the future, like a dream of what is possible, and a mental image produced by the imagination to see in your mind's eye, an unusual competence or perception and intelligent foresight. Hopeful thought reflects the belief that you can and will pursue your goals and envisioned dreams.

Positive psychologist Shane J. Lopez (2009) provided the following definition: "Hopeful [people] see the future as better than the present, and believe they have the power to make it so. These [people] are energetic and full of life. They are able to develop many strategies to reach goals and plan contingencies in the event that they are faced with problems along the way. As such, obstacles are viewed as challenges to overcome and are bypassed by garnering support and implementing alternative pathways. Perceiving the likelihood of good outcomes, these [people] focus on success and, therefore, experience greater positive affect and less distress. Generally, high-hope people experience less anxiety and less stress specific to test-taking [or other demanding situations]."

Rating: 1 2 3 4 5

Reflections:

Possible Selves

Possible selves is a conception that you can become what you see is possible. It is a thought process where you reflect upon and inquire into "what if" questions and possible scenarios for who you can become and your life direction. You believe either that you are locked into a single way of being or becoming, or that you can exercise freedom to change who you are and your life.

The possible selves attribute represents your ideas of what you might become, what you would like to become, and what you are afraid of becoming, and thus provides a conceptual link between cognition and motivation. Successful people create possible selves as a part of their growth and development.

Rating: 1 2 3 4 5

Reflections:

Self-Determination

Self-determination is defined by three needs: the need to control the course of your life (autonomy), the need to be effective in dealing with your environment (competence), and the need to have close, affectionate relationships (relatedness).

To be self-determined is to believe in your actions and experience a sense of freedom to do what is engaging and personally important. In short, you believe you can create your own destiny.

Rating: 1 2 3 4 5

Reflections:

Emotional Intelligence and Positive Emotions

Emotional intelligence is your ability to discern numerous subtle distinctions of a wide range of emotions, such as sadness and depression, happiness and elation, anger and rage. This involves the ability to manage the emotions with thought and to express them effectively and appropriately within a context. To recognize emotions in others is a quality of empathy or the ability to empathize.

Emotional intelligence consists of the capacity for each or all of these ingredients: confidence, curiosity, intentionality, self-control, relatedness, capacity to communicate, and cooperativeness (Goleman, 1995).

Positive emotions consist of episodes of pleasure, happiness, energy, confidence, positive mood, enthusiasm, love and caring, and more.

Rating: 1 2 3 4 5

Reflections:

Well-Being

Well-being refers to your psychological and physical health, where health is not simply the absence of illness, as in mental illness, but the more positive connotation of how well your life is going; your well-being is what is good for you.

Well-being includes emotional health, vitality and satisfaction, life direction and ability to make a difference, physical health and energy to function fully, healthy behaviors such as diet and exercise, quality of relationships, financial stability, experiencing a high quality of life, and living a good life.

Well-being is at the core of a lifetime of success and is imperative to a positive life trajectory. Well-being is both a self attribute and the broader desired result of self-knowledge and the purpose of a life well lived. The greater good includes the well-being of all people.

Rating: 1 2 3 4 5
Reflections:

Creativity

Creativity involves making connections between ideas or experiences that were previously unconnected. When you are being creative, you express unusual thoughts and experience life as being more interesting and stimulating. Creative people experience the world in novel and original ways, with fresh perceptions and insightful judgements, and they may make important discoveries only they can envision. These individuals often change our culture in some important way.

Everyone has the capacity for creativity. Being creative involves coming up with something new—a new idea out of nothing that is worthwhile and useful and a unique expression of you.

Rating: 1 2 3 4 5
Reflections:

Belonging

People would not be in such mental health decline if they did not need something internally: whether to emotionally fill a relationship need; feel a sense of belonging; relieve a fear of not being able to survive economically; psychologically understand the constant barrage of information and changes in the world; or to feel a spiritual connection to the greater consciousness, other human beings, and the human condition.

Therefore, if we help people develop the self-knowledge to feel more confident about being involved in a group, organization, or cause, where hope and new possibilities replace fear, people will feel that they belong. Belonging must include relating to, or identifying with, a common purpose, a higher purpose for why a particular social group exists.

Rating: 1 2 3 4 5

Reflections:

Flourishing

Without being able to focus on an internal life—feelings, self-understanding, relationship intimacy, and purpose and dreams in life, among others—it is no wonder people are experiencing that it all feels beyond their control to live a high quality, flourishing life to the level of their unique potentials and what they can envision.

Flourishing means to have a sense of self-agency or self-determination to live a high quality of life to the level of your unique potential and dreams for your life.

Rating: 1 2 3 4 5

Reflections:

Cognition

There are important cognitive processes that help you make positive changes. These include but are not limited to: the ability to think about thinking, or to see your own thought processes. Another is using your intellect or intelligence to learn and achieve. It is critical to be intellectually curious about new ideas and how these may support you and your future life course trajectories. Hoping and dreaming, for example, are both cognitive and meta-cognitive processes where you are thinking about your future possibilities.

When you are growing your mindset, you are taking in and processing new ideas that serve you, others, and the greater good for all.

Central to your psychological health is how you process information and turn that information into assumptions and beliefs. This occurs naturally and most often unconsciously. We all have cognitive models, called self-schema, that hold information representing both our internal and external beliefs, and which are critical in forming and reforming self attributes.

Examining self-destructive beliefs and belief systems and then changing these to address specific self-destructive behaviors are healthy uses of cognition. This is a good opportunity to ask yourself if you are in a growth mindset, and to what degree.

Rating: 1 2 3 4 5

Reflections:

Physical Body

What are the implications of these connections between the mind and brain physiologically? There is a growing acceptance that individuals have a significant degree of control over their own destinies in life, including their psychological and physical health, and that there is a direct connection between our psychological well-being and physical well-being. Neuroscientist Antonio Damasio affirms this view: "The fact that psychological disturbances, mild or strong, can cause disease of the body proper is finally beginning to be accepted" (Damasio, 1994).

Through time and placement in subsequent learning experiences, emotions, thinking, and actual physical responses activate or trigger the endocrine systems, the heart, blood pressure, and other biological systems that affect cognition and emotion. This integrated and dynamic relationship among brain functioning, including emotions, with bodily systems, confirms support for making the learning of the self a priority if we desire health and well-being outcomes.

This is an opportunity to fundamentally, at the being level, prevent mental and physical illness, among other desirable outcomes. One example would be to take steps to eliminate Type 2 diabetes, depression, or rotator cuff stiffness through nutrition and diet. It is critically important to reflect upon your six major body systems—digestive, circulatory, respiratory, muscular, skeletal and nervous—to determine if they are working well enough to provide the required energy to pursue your dreams for a flourishing life. Are you placing yourself in situations that empower you to

prioritize your physical health? And, are you looking inward, to your inner self to determine necessary changes?
Rating: 1 2 3 4 5
Reflections:

Dynamic connection between the self attributes

The self as the source of all possibilities is demonstrated by looking at the dynamic connection between the Integrated Self attributes described previously. When one self attribute changes, all of the attributes are changed; this occurs in the same manner as when one element of a hanging mobile structure moves freely in the air, the other elements move as well.

Observing all of the self attributes in connection reframes mental health as a capacity for flourishing and success. This reframing can generate new approaches that enhance mental health and wellness for all of us. We advocate for reframing mental health as well-being.

Self-knowledge supports and connects to all the key concepts in this book: purpose, possibilities, and transformation. Self-knowledge helps you discover your purpose, and your new perspective on your purpose can create new dreams with new possibilities. Purpose and possibilities are pathways to your transformation.

As an example, look at the Integrated Self attribute "possible selves." When you are in the process of discovering your unique purpose and vision for your life, you are encouraged to try on new selves and to conduct "what if" scenarios to see if one feels more authentic or not—more the core or real you. You may surprise yourself as you venture beyond social, family, and your own set of beliefs to find out that a more authentic self may be waiting to be discovered by you and then expressed.

Upon trying on a possible self, you may then ask whether you have the belief in yourself, as well as the belief you can make the necessary changes to your self-concept to accomplish new dreams for your life that are based upon the new sense of self. We cannot stress enough just how important it is to have a strong belief in yourself, that you can dream and manifest those dreams—"if you can dream it, you can do it" (Walt Disney).

Often when you are feeling depressed or emotionally unmotivated, you may actually have gone through a loss of hope, a loss of inspiration. When you are going through deep personal changes and transforming at your core level, you may feel all that you have built thus far in your life—all of the false beliefs you thought you were supposed to believe in and all of the circumstances in your life, such as an overemphasis upon material wealth or possessions—were for naught, and you could fall into a state of despair or hopelessness.

Some who have gone through this process call it feeling empty and meaningless. This is a temporary feeling and state of mind. You have at your core self the way forward and upward, drawing upon hope that you have a purpose that is important to express in your life, in the world. In this moment you feel happiness that you have discovered and even experienced such depth and hope—you impress yourself!

You can dream of possibilities that did not exist before, realize you have the opportunity to express what you see is possible to others, and then make these real—a beautiful experience.

Chapter 4

Connecting Your Self to Well-Being

The one common denominator we have found in all cases is that the pathway to well-being—in the eight dimensions previously described—is through a better understanding of one's self and making one's self and self-knowledge high priorities. The self is the source of possibilities. Your self and well-being are at the center of your reality, and of the creation of your reality going forward.

Reflecting on the self attributes, you have come to a more complex and sophisticated self-awareness, which provides an opportunity to create a new vision or picture of your future self. Now you have the opportunity to place each self attribute into a well-being context to honestly assess and determine opportunities to grow and change personally and professionally.

Success in life requires psychological well-being. Harvard psychologist Dr. Shawn Achor's research demonstrates that only 25% of our success comes from the intellect. The remaining 75% is divided among optimism levels and social supports, and the ability to see stress as a challenge instead of a threat. "If we change our formula for happiness and success, we can change our realities" (Achor, 2010). Further, only 10% of our external circumstances predict our future success, which means that 90% stems from the lens through which we see the world and create our realities, from the inside out.

These findings support the heart of our own research and work on developing well-being through teaching self-knowledge and possibilities for all people. We have developed methods you are learning in this book that empower you to create a new self that allows you to re-envision the formula for your success to include attributes such as happiness, optimism, purpose, and building your own meaningful networks of support.

Personal success is a state of mind consisting of happiness, finding meaning, contributing to others, having the ability to form deep and meaningful relationships, cultivating unique talents, and the energy and motivation to accomplish.

The psychological well-being factors

We have learned that the vast majority of people are not aware of what mental health and well-being are.

Mental health is not mental illness; they are two very different and distinct paradigms of understanding your own or another's psychological state of mind or condition. According to the World Health Organization (WHO), mental health is "a state of well-being in which the individual realizes his or her own abilities, can cope with the normal stresses of life, can work productively and fruitfully, and is able to make a contribution to his or her community." It is important to note mental health is a "state of well-being" that allows an individual to see and achieve their own unique potentials in life, and not simply the absence of mental illness.

Our usual way of thinking and talking about mental health is that something needs to be wrong—with a deep concern about an internal state such as depression, anxiety, suicide ideation, feelings of anger, or social behaviors where another is abused or demeaned. Often, we are not aware that just going through the motions in living daily life in a state of numbness or not living up to our own sense of human potential—meaning not using all of our natural gifts fully— are also indicators of lacking mental health. Said another way, mental health is not simply the absence of mental health symptoms.

From the field of positive psychology and Dr. Carolyn Ryff's work in particular, we know that mental health and well-being can be viewed on a scale, from -5 to 0 to +5. Typically, people with mental illness are assessed in the negative side of this scale, while mental health and well-being are assessed on the positive side. We begin to flourish when our psychological well-being is above 0.

Psychological well-being is a state of mind where individuals have:

- Autonomy. Individuals are independent and regulate their behavior independent of social pressures. An example statement for this criterion is, "I have confidence in my opinions, even if they are contrary to the general consensus."
  Some examples of related Integrated Self attributes are: Locus of Control, Self-Efficacy, and Self-Understanding.

- Circumstantial mastery. Individuals make effective use of opportunities and have a sense of mastery in

managing external circumstances, factors and activities, including managing everyday affairs and creating situations to benefit personal needs. An example statement for this criterion is, "In general, I feel I am in charge of the situation in which I live."
Some examples of related Integrated Self attributes are: Self-Esteem, Self-Determination, Cognition.

- Personal growth. Individuals continue to develop, welcome new experiences, recognize improvements in behavior, have the ability to "experience their experiences" such as feelings, and increase their understanding of self over time. An example statement for this criterion is, "I think it is important to have new experiences that challenge how I think about myself and the world."
Some examples of related Integrated Self attributes are: Possible Selves, Identity, and Self-Concept.

- Positive relations with others. Individuals engage in meaningful relationships with others that include reciprocal empathy, intimacy, and affection. An example statement for this criterion is, "People would describe me as a giving person, willing to share my gifts with others."
Some examples of related Integrated Self attributes are: Self-Affect, Self Esteem, and Belonging.

- Purpose in life. Individuals strive for a deeper understanding of why they are here, possess a strong giving orientation and conviction that life holds

meaning, and want to contribute to the greater good. An example statement for this criterion is, "Some people wander aimlessly through life, but I am not one of them."
Some examples of related Integrated Self attributes are: Life Meaning; Life Purpose and Spirituality; and Inspiration, Hope, and Dreams.

- Self-knowledge. Individuals have a positive attitude about their inner life and self, and an innate curiosity or motivation to understand who they are with multiple dimensions. An example statement for this criterion is, "I like the path I am on and who I am becoming."
All of the Integrated Self attributes are related to Self-Knowledge.

- Holistic health. Individuals feel healthy, emotionally, psychologically, and physically, and they have the level of energy, motivation, and hope to manifest their higher purpose and dreams for a better life.
Some examples of related Integrated Self attributes are: Happiness, Physical Body, and Flourishing.

The following Reflection enables you to assess yourself in these mental health and well-being factors. If in any one of the factors you assess you are not fully functioning to your own standards, then this is an opportunity to take the necessary action. Know that if you do take action to improve any one or combination of criteria, then you will benefit—it is to your own advantage.

~ REFLECTION ~
Your personal connection to the psychological well-being factors

Create a personal connection to the psychological well-being factors. On a scale of one to five, with five representing a high score or strength, rate yourself in each of the well-being factors. Then, describe which factor could be a special strength on which to build your future success:

Autonomy. You are self-determining and independent; able to resist social pressures to think and act in certain ways; regulate your behavior from within; and evaluate yourself by personal standards.
Rating: 1 2 3 4 5

Environmental mastery. You have a sense of mastery and competence in managing your environment; control a complex array of external activities; make effective use of surrounding opportunities; and are able to choose or create contexts suitable to personal needs and values.
Rating: 1 2 3 4 5

Personal growth. You gain a feeling of continued development; see yourself as growing and expanding; are open to new experiences; have a sense of realizing your potential; see improvement in yourself and your behavior over time; and are changing in ways that reflect more self-knowledge and effectiveness.
Rating: 1 2 3 4 5

Positive relations with others. You are able to have warm, satisfying, trusting relationships with others; are concerned about the welfare of others; are capable of strong empathy, affection, and intimacy; and understand the give and take of human relationships.
Rating: 1 2 3 4 5

Purpose in life. You experience a connection to your spirituality and dreams in life; have a sense of direction; feel there is meaning to present and past life experiences; hold beliefs that give life purpose; and have aims and objectives for living.
Rating: 1 2 3 4 5

Self-knowledge. You possess a positive attitude toward yourself; acknowledge and accept multiple aspects of yourself, including good and bad qualities; and feel positive about previous life experiences.
Rating: 1 2 3 4 5

Holistic health. You feel healthy, emotionally, psychologically, and physically, and have the level of energy, motivation, and hope to manifest your purpose and dreams for a better life.
Rating: 1 2 3 4 5

Choose one of the previous well-being factors that is one of your strengths, and describe how it can help build your future success:

Choose another factor that offers an opportunity for growth, and describe how it can help you to explore new possibilities:

Your ability to grow and change

People of all ages—children, adolescents, young adults, and adults—need to learn how to change their beliefs when necessary, to create a better future for themselves and toward the greater good for all. The inability to change one's beliefs is a symptom of psychological condition known as a "fixed mindset."

The field of positive psychology indicates that someone with a fixed mindset has the aim to achieve validation. The person constantly tries to prove themselves and is highly sensitive to being wrong or making a mistake. Failure brings the person doubt, demeans their character, and destroys their confidence. As a result, a person with a fixed mindset always feels anxious and is vulnerable to setbacks or criticisms and feels powerless in the world. Resulting behaviors include bullying, aggressiveness toward others, demeaning those who represent different views, and letting off steam or expressing inappropriately just to release the stress and anxiety that build.

The ability to develop "resilience" is fast becoming an important personal quality to live a good life. Resilience is the process of adapting well in the face of adversity, trauma, tragedy, threats, or even significant sources of stress—such as family and relationship problems, serious health problems, or academic and financial stressors. It means "bouncing back" from difficult experiences.

A combination of factors contributes to resilience. The primary factor in resilience is having self-knowledge which includes purpose in life.

School-aged children, adolescents, and young adults with self-awareness and psychological well-being have a lower risk of mental health disorders and physical health diagnoses, such as anxiety, depression, obesity, cutting, substance abuse, and bullying, among others. As such, self-knowledge is an important protective factor to impart in a young adult's life in preparation for college and careers. To experience self—the whole self—is the height of socio-emotional capacity and the most important protective factor to impart to children, adolescents, young adults, and all adults throughout a lifespan.

Chapter 5

Completing Obstacles to Growth: Regrets and Resentments

In this chapter, you will be experiencing many emotions—this is good. Do not censure or repress your emotions, and do not judge them. If you are sad because someone did not love you in a particular way, your sadness is legitimate and real and okay. You will be going to a deeper level of understanding about what has kept you from seeing possibilities in your life and to creating new experiences that are more along the lines of what you want and can envision.

You will, or have already asked yourself, why you are not achieving or realizing what seems like, to you, relatively small and simple goals. It may seem to you like you are stuck, or at least not moving forward toward a better life and the one you want. Repressed emotions are often behind what keeps you stuck and not growing. Most often there are two emotions that create the biggest blocks to growing our conscious awareness of who we are and our future potentials: anger and sadness.

When reading this chapter, you may think allowing these thoughts and feelings to arise is not justified; your life is going along just fine, and you are relatively OK. However, when you *do* allow yourself to get in touch with the widest range of emotions possible, you are honoring your core self, and communicating to yourself you are worth it to feel deeply and completely. Take small steps, then as you go through your Reflections and through daily life, more and more recollections of incidences will arise. This is a healthy process. Do not stop yourself from feeling your feelings; they are your own and are very personal to you.

George Bernard Shaw said, "People are always blaming their circumstances for what they are. I don't believe in circumstances. The people who get on in the world are the people who get up and look for the circumstances they want, and if they can't find them, make them." Allowing yourself to recall and fully feel emotions about past events will empower you to complete the emotions, move forward beyond the circumstances, and create the future.

Actor and film producer Will Smith described the difference between fault and responsibility: "As long as we're pointing the finger and stuck in whose fault something is, we're jammed and trapped into victim mode. And when you're in victim mode, you're stuck and suffering. ... The road to power is in taking responsibility. Your heart, your life, and your happiness are your responsibility and your responsibility alone" (2018).

Life happens to you at an unconscious level, it comes at you from birth to death. You go through numerous experiences in your life, many you are aware of, with others you do not remember consciously—but somewhere you can remember, as even your muscles store experiences in your body. You are somewhere in the middle, transitioning from one stage of life to the next one. Transitions by definition are characterized by change, some at the surface level, and others at deeper being, character, or personality levels.

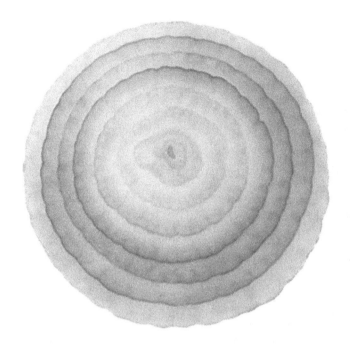

The experiences and events in your life layer in your mind like the layers of a sliced onion, as depicted above. For your understanding and use in the following Reflection, consider that you have lived life from birth to present day, and in each moment of each day you have experienced various events, which are made up of circumstances, feelings, interpretations, and assumptions. Some are major events, while others pass by without much notice or even memory. Others, such as traumatic events, are omnipresent in their impact upon your psyche, your psychological state of mind. At the center of the onion are your early life's experiences, while the outer layers are closer to present day or recent experiences.

~ REFLECTION ~
Regrets

Reflect upon your entire life, birth to present, to recall the experiences that were the most impactful in your life. Remember, *you* decide which are and are not.

Go through each experience and determine if you have any regrets.

If you feel uncomfortable doing this and the next Reflection, this is normal and expected. If this gets too intense, take a break, meditate with deep breathing to clear your mind, or take a walk before returning to the Reflection. And if you are in crisis, seek out professional help as soon as possible.

Definition of Regret:
> A troubled feeling or remorse over something that has happened, especially over something that you have done or left undone.

Remorse:
> A deep, torturing sense of guilt felt over a wrong that you have done; self-reproach (i.e., blaming yourself).

Regret Process

In your life, locate something you regret, and answer the following questions:

1. Exactly what did you do or not do that you regret?
2. When did you do it or not do it?

3. What part of what you did (or didn't do) can you be responsible for doing (or not doing)?
4. What other part of what you did (or didn't do) are you willing to be responsible for doing (or not doing)?
5. Repeat item 4 until you feel a sense of completion about this regret.
6. What is the *unconscious benefit* you gain in regretting it instead of clearing it up, handling it, or letting it be? The unconscious benefit is something you get to avoid, such as not having to admit you were wrong about something, or having to take a new risk in life. It is sometimes hard to see, but it is there.
7. What does it *cost* you not to clear it up, handle it, or let it be?
8. Please get in touch with the appropriate emotion and intensity of that emotion; for example, if you are sad, then express the regret with sadness.
9. Communicate to others the regrets in your life first in this book or your journal, then in a letter you may or may not choose to send, and then in person, if you feel compelled and have determined it is safe for you and the other individual(s) involved.
10. State to yourself, "I am willing to complete and release this regret."
11. Repeat items 1 through 10 until you have completed all of the major regrets you can recall in your life.

Use this space for reflections:

~ REFLECTION ~
Resentments

Review impactful life experiences and determine if you have any resentments.

Definition of Resentment:
> A feeling of bitter hurt or indignation, from a sense of being injured or offended, emotionally, psychologically, and physically. Indignation or ill will felt as a result of a real or imagined grievance (see Anger).

Resent:
> To feel bitter hurt or indignation at some act or remark or toward a person from a sense of being injured or offended.

Anger:
> A strong emotion you feel when you think that someone has behaved in an unfair, cruel, or unacceptable way.

Resentment Process

In your life, locate a specific person toward whom you have a resentment, and answer the following questions:

1. What happened?
2. When did it happen?
3. Where did it happen?

4. Exactly what happened that you resented?
5. With respect to this situation, what haven't you communicated?
6. To whom didn't you communicate that?
7. If they were here right now, exactly what would you say to them?
8. Get in touch with the appropriate emotion and intensity of that emotion.
9. After completing this process for all of your resentments you can recall, communicate with others until you have expressed yourself fully and are complete. As in expressing regrets, first journal your thoughts and feelings, write a letter to send or not to a specific person, and then, if you feel compelled, communicate in person, if you have determined it is safe for you and the other individual(s).
10. State to yourself, "I am willing to complete and release this resentment."
11. Repeat items 1 through 10 until you are complete on all of your resentments at this time.

Use this space for reflections:

Chapter 6

Listening to Your Deeper Self through Mindful Meditation

The Reflections in this chapter provide the opportunity to do your own mindfulness exercise, through a self-guided meditation. This is actually such a fun and rewarding and deeply satisfying meditation. Each time you visit this mindful place, keep in mind all of the self attributes learned thus far, and note your growth in accessing your source of power, your inner self.

You will be engaging in positive self-talk. You are communicating with your deepest levels of consciousness, the subconscious and intuition. Your unconscious mind always says "yes" to what your conscious mind says. So, it is in your self-interest to ask or assert positive thoughts so that you gain agreement and support from your unconscious mind. Further, you may find yourself asking these type of questions as you go about your daily activities, as a form of mindful meditation.

The size or space of your listening is the size of the possibilities open to you.

~ REFLECTION ~
Asking questions of your inner self

Questions open up the size of your listening and provide access to your inner self.

Questions about advice, analysis, friends, career, relationships, and insights are often good kinds of questions to ask when you want to open yourself up to deeper levels of knowing.

Some examples:

"What actions can I take to . . . ?"
"How can I better . . . ?"
"What is a good way of approaching . . . ?"
"What is my next step in . . . ?"

Questions to ask yourself should require more than a "yes" or "no" answer. This will give you an opportunity to communicate verbally with your inner self. A "yes" or "no" answer does not give much of a chance for extended communication.

At this time, write down three (3) questions of your own about anything you want to know about.

1.

2.

3.

Pause

Please stop here and allow yourself time to reflect upon your questions. Take as much time as you require—minutes, hours, days or more.

~ REFLECTION ~
Going deeper using mindful meditation

You have the power to listen to your inner self, at your deepest level. You can access this deepest inner place in the technique you are about to do. At this time, formally *choose* to go to this deeper place by saying, "I choose to go to a deeper place within myself; I choose to know myself at a deeper level."

Please read the following three paragraphs slowly and deliberately. Read them several times so you can recall the steps when your eyes are closed. Next, breathe deeply for a few moments and relax your entire body. Then close your eyes for this guided meditation:

Imagine yourself walking down a clear path through a beautiful forest area. It is a safe place to just let yourself go, to let your thoughts wander freely. You are alone and feel very safe and protected.

You see in front of you in the distance a small and beautiful house or other welcoming structure. You are drawn to this magical place by some powerful force, a very bright light that does not hurt your eyes to look at; in fact, it feels good to look at it. It draws you closer, and closer, and closer. You want to get closer and closer to the brilliant, bright light. The closer you get to the source of the light, the better you feel inside.

You are now only a few feet away from the source of the brilliant light, and you see a teacher or mentor whom you love and trust and who wishes you well . . . you are now only inches away from this guide, who asks you for your three questions. Listen with an open mind to whatever your guide communicates.

Open your eyes and write down the answers to your three questions now:

1.

2.

3.

Reflect upon the answers. The specifics of what you saw are not of great importance: your teacher may turn out to be someone you don't know, someone you do know, or even just an energy form or presence, and you may meet any place from a small cottage to a beautiful house of worship. Picture whatever works well for you. And, it may be different *each time* you do this Reflection.

After doing this technique, answer the following questions to yourself and then, if you would like, interact about them with one other person who is fully supportive of your inquiry:

1. Were the questions and answers ones that you would have expected?

2. Which answers were helpful?

3. What was the source of the light?

As you go about your daily life, be present to your experiences—or said another way, fully "experience your experiences"—as they are powerfully rich and beautiful and full of meaning and joy!

Chapter 7

Transforming Your Consciousness

You will reach a peak or a high point to your experiences in Chapters 7 and 8 through completing The Success Predictor, a framework we developed in which you put together the DNA of your consciousness, the various levels of your whole self, and the future you can imagine and thus create. You will align your highest calling, with your purpose in life, with what you see is possible for you and humanity, with direct pathways to implement these in the world and in your life. This is hard, deep work and worth every effort. You will see and experience a whole new you either immediately or throughout The Success Predictor process—truly exciting!

You will engage in a consciousness-raising, transformative experience as you read and apply The Success Predictor to your own life.

The Success Predictor is a highly effective framework used by parents, teachers, and school, college, career, professional development, and psychological counselors to help guide people of all ages, developmental stages, and walks of life toward their highest expressions of what is possible for them. It is used to assess, diagnose, and intervene into the mindset of people who want to see and achieve their full and unique potentials in life, and then empower them to succeed and manifest their full and unique potentials.

The Success Predictor is a framework for your personal and professional development, to determine who you are and those pathways that will lead to your definition of success. The framework requires that you determine your *own* definitions of success and achievement by listening to your thoughts and feelings.

The Success Predictor is used to: determine internal motivations to succeed, understand reference points of capabilities, diagnose internal states of well-being, develop empowering family cultures, formulate career aspirations, determine professional acumen, understand academic program interests, guide life and career directions, understand personal paradigms of reality, and guide interventions, among others. The Success Predictor is used to help guide you in making a transformation from the person you think you are supposed to be, to the person you know you are meant to be.

Learning about who you are and how to create a great life with numerous possible experiences offers a special opportunity, possibly for the first time in your life, to reflect upon, "Who am I now?" and "How have my life circumstances shaped me to be the person I am supposed to be?"

These circumstances may be family values, childhood traumas, traditions, behaviors, and dominant cultural forces—such as social media, the prevalence of prescription drug abuse, mass school shootings, and global warming, among others. You can reflect on, "Who am I meant to be?" Special and unique is the opportunity to consider your life purpose. "Do I have a calling in life, repressed dreams for my life?" and "What is meaningful to me?" are among the important questions to ask at this developmental and transitional stage.

How The Success Predictor works

As we wrote in the introduction, emotions motivate us to grow and make a difference in the real world. Without emotions and motivated reasoning, change is not possible. When you know what you want and are passionate about it, structural tension is created. Structural tension is the energy created when an individual concurrently envisions a desired future state, while being completely aware of the limitations of current reality. The difference between the desired future state and current reality creates a tension that seeks resolution toward one or the other.

The idea of structural tension applies the first axiom of structural dynamics (Fritz, 1984, Jung, 1972, Odum, 1988) to individual change. The archetypal psychologist Carl Jung described the unconscious structural dynamic as a natural driving force within us—an ecosystem of consciousness. Howard Odem's application of structural dynamics demonstrates how inertia is accelerated given states of tension. Robert Fritz took this idea and demonstrated how to apply it to human development with the use of a manipulative, the rubber band, which helps to make this idea experiential. In the following paragraphs, we put these concepts together into an integrated holistic process.

In any transformation process, it is critical to establish this structural tension in order to empower positive change. When this tension is created, emotional thought drives the change process. As a human being who wants to grow and change, it is your responsibility to learn how to establish this structural tension in your daily life, and not have to rely upon parents, professional counselors, or other experts. Of course, please use these experts if they can help facilitate your growth, development, or mastery in using the methods in this book.

Please get a rubber band for demonstration purposes. The concept of structural tension can be better understood with the use of the rubber band. Place one end of the rubber band in your left hand, and call that current reality; then, place the other end of the rubber band in your right hand, and call that future vision.

The Success Predictor uses the dynamic that tension seeks resolution (figure below). This initiates the change process—the emotional desire to attain a future state, a goal, a dream. This dynamic is essential for all to understand and apply to their lives, careers, and well-being.

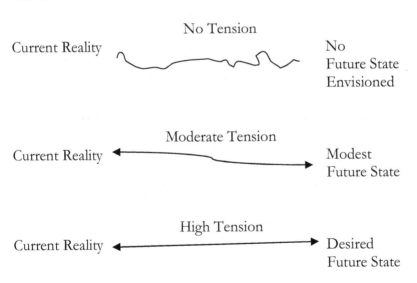

No Tension

Current Reality   No
Future State
Envisioned

Moderate Tension

Current Reality   Modest
Future State

High Tension

Current Reality   Desired
Future State

The previous figure presents three levels of tension between the left side, current reality, and the right side, the degree to which a future state is desired. The first level is "No Tension," which indicates you are just going through the motions, floating through life, allowing circumstances to dictate direction, feelings, and sense of self, with very little commitment toward anyone or anything, including self and personal growth and development. Additionally, you may not have a clear picture of present reality, either emotional states or physical situation.

The second level, "Moderate Tension," indicates a modest commitment to a desired future state, most often with the ability to envision general circumstances such as more money, a new car, or new relationships. Most likely, if this is where you are, you are not able to envision a future state that includes emotions or to feel as an important part of the quality of life. You are most likely not very clear about your present emotional state.

The third level, "High Tension," indicates the ability to dream about a complete and whole picture that includes emotional states of being, who you want to become (e.g., a healthy person who makes a difference), and numerous and clear distinctions about both emotional and circumstantial future realities. You are also able to clearly identify current emotional states, even if they include sadness or frustration that the future state is yet to be realized. You are also clearer about your unique potential in life—something special you have to give or contribute to others and or the world.

The self mediates and is the go-between or corridor that connects the social with the personal, the external with the internal, and the present with the future. This is why we went so deeply into understanding the 30 attributes in the

Integrated Self Model—the self shapes all important pathways.

The growth cycle in all human beings begins with a natural phenomenon that tension must be created and that it seeks resolution. People create themselves and their own realities, futures, and well-being.

Out of this natural event comes an energy or force which propels you toward your chosen result. This force is generated from the natural movement of tension toward resolution. If you stretch a rubber band, it tends to seek resolution of the structural tension you have created. As it moves toward resolution, it releases energy. In a somewhat similar way, you can learn to create structural tension in your consciousness. As your consciousness moves toward resolution, it generates and releases energy which is used in the actual process of moving from where you are to where you want to be.

When this principle is used properly, results often seem to occur effortlessly and easily. It is even common for people to report the phenomenon of results occurring "as if by magic!"

This tension can be resolved in one of two ways (or some combination of the two):

1. The tension can be resolved through a change in your vision, so that it comes to correspond more closely with current reality. In other words, by deciding, "Things aren't so bad" or "I guess I really don't want that after all," you give up your vision, reduce the structural tension, and don't get the result you really want.

2. The tension can be resolved through a change in reality, so that your outward circumstances come to correspond more closely with your vision. In other words, the structural tension is resolved by having what you want.

The degree to which you hold the vision clearly is the degree to which the tension will tend to resolve in favor of that vision.

Creating structural tension gets you what you want

"Structural tension" and "psychological tension" are, when understood, significantly different. The tension we are speaking about is structural tension. It is not psychological tension, which is the experience of anxiety, depression, conflict, or physiological or psychological stress.

It is common for people to convert structural tension into psychological tension. This comes from a lack of appreciation for discrepancy and an intolerance for situations in which present reality is not the way it is wanted. This is the premise upon which the entire psychology profession is built.

Effectively creating results *comes from cultivating structural tension rather than avoiding it.* It is important to note the difference between psychological and structural tension, because in your transformation process you will be using structural tension, while simultaneously contributing to an experience of relaxation, balance, and inner peace.

Since structural tension results from a discrepancy between what you want (vision) and what you now have (current reality), the best way to cultivate structural tension is to:

- *Be clear about what you now want (vision).*
  If you experience psychological tension or conflict about not having what you want, you might be tempted to cut your dreams down to "realistic proportions" and "not try for so much" or go for new possibilities. By lowering your vision in this way, you would be decreasing the structural tension, thus making it far less likely you would get what you truly want and manifest what is possible for you. If, instead, you continue to hold a vision of what you actually want—even if you are a bit uncomfortable doing so—structural tension is maintained and powerful energy is released which will aid you in creating it.

- *Be clear about what you now have (current reality).*
  Another way you may be tempted to avoid or attempt to resolve psychological tension associated with not having what you want is to obscure or misrepresent current reality by telling yourself, "It's really not so bad" (a false positive thinking), or by ignoring unpleasant facts which would make you uncomfortable if you faced them. You might even go so far as to lie to yourself about the true state of affairs, telling yourself you are doing fine when you actually are not. Once again, such strategies would tend to weaken structural tension and reduce your chances of having what you want.

When you are in the transformation process to create the life you want, you want to know current reality, even if you are disappointed or uncomfortable at what you see. In the transformation process, *current reality is essential feedback you need* to contribute to structural tension. Structural tension helps bring you the results you desire.

> Example:
> *You have a vision of a "wonderful job," which includes expressing your talents and abilities, working with creative people in a stimulating atmosphere, and making a comfortable salary. The current reality is that you are unemployed. Creating structural tension involves noticing the reality of your jobless situation, holding a vision of the job you desire, and allowing the discrepancy between your reality and your vision to exist.*

Structural tension exists as the inherent difference between your vision (having a great job) and your reality (unemployment).

Psychological tension could exist if you become tense or anxious about your jobless situation. By appreciating the discrepancy between current reality and your vision, without reducing it artificially to avoid any discomfort you may feel, you will tend to resolve the discrepancy in favor of the vision.

~ REFLECTION ~
Creating structural tension
between your vision and reality

1. What do you tend to do when structural tension is present in your life?

2. What do you want?

3. What is your current situation (your current reality)?

~ REFLECTION ~
How to discover your higher purpose and what is possible for your life

The Success Predictor is a framework to be completed by you as you are searching for what is next, in life transitions, relationships, family, school and career changes, and personal development through a crisis, among others. The framework helps you understand who you are and are meant to be.

Before completing The Success Predictor, it is important to read and become familiar with the categories and their definitions used in the framework. Definitions are provided to assist you in formulating a personal connection to the category. To complete The Success Predictor framework, understand that each category is a level of your consciousness, your own knowing about you and the way you frame your reality. Therefore, it is important you take each category and develop a personal experience of it, or derive personal meaning.

Please view the 10 categories as a hierarchy of levels of understanding. These categories are not yet ordered by level, therefore please organize them by level, much like solving a puzzle. This will assist in the transformation of how you organize your own view of reality and self. You may need to make a number of attempts to organize the categories to solve the puzzle. There is no absolute correct puzzle solution, but we will show you in a few pages the most accurate representation of the hierarchy of consciousness.

Levels of understanding means that each category is a subset of the previous, higher category. For example, the category "purpose" requires a higher level of understanding, or broader view, than does "plans," as one example. Therefore, when placing the category "purpose" in your hierarchy, please consider your level of understanding and view.

The Success Predictor categories

Here are the 10 Success Predictor categories listed in random order. After reading their definitions, put the categories in hierarchical order:

Category   Definition

Results   Evidence that you are on the right track toward manifesting your purpose, vision, goals, and plans; a compass; what is left after you take action.

Mission   An inner calling to pursue an activity or perform a service; a vocation; the area of life where you will manifest your purpose.

Commitments   What you are determined to do; a pledge to do; a state of being bound emotionally or intellectually to someone or something, like a strong belief.

Being

The essence of a human being; the totality of all things that exist; the qualities that constitute existence or essence; your basic nature.

Tactics

Step-by-step actions to take to implement the plans; a series of steps toward achieving a goal or implementing a plan.

Goals

To accomplish something by a certain time; "what by when."

Vision

What you can see in the future, like a dream of what is possible; a mental image produced by the imagination, to see in your mind's eye; unusual competence or perception; intelligent foresight.

Strategies

An approach to take, or method to use to accomplish a specific goal; how you will manifest your goals; approaches or alternatives.

Plans

To form a scheme or program for the accomplishment of a goal; to make a graphic representation, like a blueprint; how you will execute the strategies formulated.

Purpose

The reason why you are here, for your existence; raison d'être; describes or connects with your basic nature or being.

101

Please use this space (or additional pages in a separate journal) to make numerous attempts at organizing your understanding of the 10 categories into a contextual hierarchy.

Pause

Please do not go to the next section of The Success Predictor process until you have organized the puzzle pieces for yourself, arranged them in a meaningful contextual hierarchy, and then confirmed your understanding. By organizing your own contextual hierarchy, you are creating for yourself your own understanding, and this will help you gain more insight when you complete The Success Predictor. Our representation of the hierarchy is revealed next. Now turn the page to see whether your contextual hierarchy is similar.

The Success Predictor™

Contextual Hierarchy

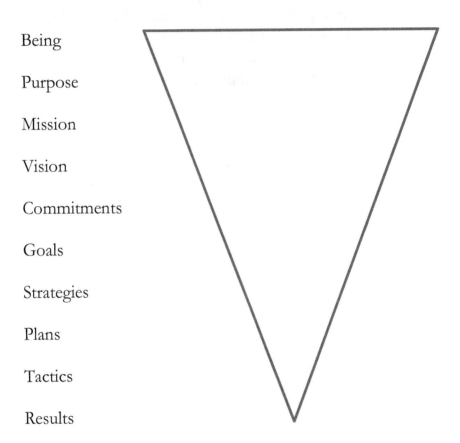

Being

Purpose

Mission

Vision

Commitments

Goals

Strategies

Plans

Tactics

Results

The triangle represents that each category is a subset of the previous, higher category.

Chapter 8

Creating Your Purpose and Future Possibilities: The Success Predictor

In this chapter you have the opportunity to directly apply each of the 10 Success Predictor categories to you and your life—literally creating your future! This is serious and hard work, yet simultaneously invigorating and exciting.

When you have completed the framework, you will have a snapshot or present picture of who you are and your view of your reality, self, and future success, so please consider your responses carefully and consciously.

Your responses in each category may be written or drawn. Often, people completing The Success Predictor take pictures from magazines, websites, or their camera and paste them into a what is popularly called a "dream journal." These pictures assist in clarifying what each level of understanding looks and feels like, especially the vision and results levels.

~ REFLECTION ~
Create your own Success Predictor

Being

Being is your existence or your connection to all human beings at a higher level of consciousness. It can be understood as God-given or spiritual. Your soul—bigger, more expansive, and more powerful than your mind or body—connects you to your being.

Use this space to reflect on your sense of spiritual connection to all humanity. Then turn the page to begin to build your Success Predictor and your flourishing future.

Additional space …

The "why" contextual levels of understanding

Purpose

Your purpose is the reason why you are here, in this life. It is what you commit your life to, bigger than yourself, using your unique talents, values, and vision in the service of creating a better world. It is part of the underlying motivation and driving force which guides your actions and brings fulfillment. Your purpose engages a lifelong process that you can continuously discover and improve upon, and it compels you to make a difference in your life, the lives of others, and the condition of the world.

The following George Bernard Shaw quote characterizes the spirit of a person's purpose: "This is the true joy in life, the being used for a purpose recognized by yourself as a mighty one; the being a force of nature instead of a feverish selfish little clod of ailments and grievances complaining that the world will not devote itself to making you happy. I want to be thoroughly used up when I die, for the harder I work the more I live. I rejoice in life for its own sake. Life is no 'brief candle' to me. It is a sort of splendid torch which I have got hold of for the moment, and I want to make it burn as brightly as possible before handing it on to future generations" (Man and Superman, 1973).

You will want to understand your purpose so it can guide your personal development, mental health and well-being, friendships, romantic and family relationships, academic studies, career direction, and then help you to design a life course strategy that communicates your self-understanding and the difference you would like to make in the world.

To arrive at your purpose, use your dreams or visions for the life that you want to live and the world you want to create. Your dreams and visions are what you see that are important to you; honor your dreams. Another way to think about your purpose and arrive at an understanding is to think about what issues and concerns in the world you are drawn to, that are important to you and evoke emotions. A third way to discover your purpose is to listen to your deepest self, to that voice in your head that is the voice of your conscience, what the Greeks called your "daimon" (pronounced dī'-mōn, the original Greek meaning is an attendant spirit, a genius). Your daimon is that voice, your guiding spirit that will guide you to know what your God-given purpose is. Sometimes, your purpose is found through tragedy—something that happened to you in your childhood, such as a traumatic event like experiencing physical or sexual abuse, parental alcoholism or drug abuse, or other family dynamics that impacted you.

In short, your life's experiences will speak to you when you are open to listening for what your purpose might be. You will most likely not be clear the first pass or attempt. It may take a number of attempts, as your sit with this category and go on living daily life, to notice what emerges, what you are thinking and feeling.

Helpful Hint: Here are some characteristics of an effective purpose statement:

1. Clear and concise, no longer than one to five sentences.
2. Present tense, e.g., "I make a difference in everything that I do."
3. Simple to understand and remember.
4. Congruent with your values and vision.
5. Includes "why" and the "who" or "what" you positively impact.
6. Refers to a lifelong process that can never be totally obtained or outlived.
7. Can be accomplished through your effort.
8. Compels you to act with passion, energy, and commitment.
9. Is a unique expression of you.
10. Is inspirational to you (and possibly to others).

My Purpose is:

Mission

When you have a mission in life, you feel an inner calling to pursue an activity or to perform a service for humankind. This is sometimes a gut feeling, your intuition speaking, and is important to listen to. Your mission represents the pathway you take through a domain to manifest your purpose. Your mission is something you know you are meant to do in service of creating a better world. Along with your purpose, it is part of the underlying motivation and driving force which guides your actions and brings fulfillment.

Some people—religious leaders, teachers, doctors, therapists—may hear a vocational calling that is directly connected to their life purpose. One central question to ask in formulating your mission is "where" in the world you will manifest your purpose: "Where is my calling needed by others?" Here are examples of mission statements: "I serve adolescents by helping them feel emotional safety and healing, and I make it easier for them to love one another as the leader of a school," and "I create a healthy, happy and flourishing family by learning about human development and bringing mindfulness into my family culture."

Understanding your mission will help guide your selection of academic areas of study to be trained professionally to help reach those who need your calling, as well as design a life course strategy that communicates your self-understanding and the difference you would like to make in the world.

Referencing the first mission statement example, an adult in transition would make plans to study adolescent psychology, pastoral counseling, or education, and then begin to develop professional opportunities in educational settings. While you may choose to align with an organization's mission, your mission is personal and a part of you no matter where you are employed or volunteering.

Areas in which to consider contributing your mission often are: family, profession, career, your own health and wellness, friendships, marriage, community organizations, politics, and non-profit philanthropy, among numerous others.

Helpful Hint: Here are some characteristics of an effective mission statement:

1. Clear and concise; no longer than five to seven sentences.
2. Present tense, e.g., "I am a teacher of emotional healing through families and schools."
3. Congruent with your purpose and vision.
4. Includes "who" or "what" you positively impact, and "where" in the world.
5. Speaks to your own understanding of your inner calling.
6. Is meaningful to you.
7. Is a unique expression of you.

My Mission is:

The Success Predictor

The "what" contextual levels of understanding

Vision

You can create your future. Many of us plod along day after day, living as if we are simply playing out roles in a play that is already written for us. That play has *not* been written. You must create it through a vision of your ideal future. Vision is the design of your own destiny in life; it is your dream of what you want your life to be. A clear understanding of your vision answers two questions: "What will I be doing?" (activities) and "What will I feel like?" (energy).

It is usually easy to imagine the activities and tasks you will be doing and the success you will be enjoying from doing those tasks. It is sometimes more difficult to imagine your energy, what personal and relationship behaviors, attitudes, and character traits you will be living by in order to produce the results you want.

Your vision is what you see is possible for you, for the world, and for your contributions and accomplishments. When formulating a vision or dream, do not ask, "Is this realistic?"; for if you are creating your own destiny, you decide if your dreams become a reality or not.

You will want to understand your vision so it can guide your life choices and propel you toward your future self. Your vision can help you to reach those who need your calling, and then to design life and career strategies that communicate your self-understanding and your vision for a better life and world.

Helpful Hint: Here are some characteristics of an effective vision statement:

1. Present tense, e.g., "I am challenged every day in my work with children and energized by the contributions I know I am making to make certain that children do not suffer in the world."
2. Includes specific action details rather than broad generalities, e.g., "I volunteer one night per week at the hospital and experience a sense of belonging," versus "I serve others."
3. Combines both what you are doing (activity or task) and how you are feeling when doing it (energy).
4. Includes information about all aspects of your future: school, family, relationships, work, spiritual, social, physical, emotional, financial, others.
5. Congruent with your values, life purpose, and mission.
6. It should be something you really want, not something you should want.
7. Formulated by you, in fact created by you based upon your own inner sense of what is possible for *you*! Note, not your parents, siblings, or others in your life.

My Vision is: (To represent your vision, please feel free to use written words, drawings, and pictures in a separate journal, taking all the space you need. This is popularly known as your "dream journal.")

Commitments

Commitment is the triumph of possibility over resignation, of creating your life's destiny versus having it determined for you by others. Your commitments empower you to step beyond what is comfortable or predictable, beyond the limits you thought you had—toward a dynamic and challenging life of active contribution and self-expression. Your commitments are what you believe in, your ground, or stand.

Your commitment is what you have pledged to do, to take a stand for, for you, for the world, and for your contributions and accomplishments. When determining your set of commitments, do not ask, "Will my commitments help me become famous?" Your commitments are your own deeply held beliefs, regardless of the affirmation of others.

You will want to understand your commitments so they can guide your life choices, personal characteristics, psychological and emotional well-being, relationships, academic studies, career direction, and family decisions, and make your vision a reality through a life that is an expression of your self-understanding. Your commitments should be expressed in every communication and action in every part of your life.

Helpful Hint: Here are some characteristics of an effective commitment statement:

1. Present tense, e.g., "I am committed to making my purpose manifest in the world through musical performance."
2. Includes specific belief details rather than broad generalities, e.g., "I believe in the power of musical performance to transform people's experiences of goodness in the world," versus "I love music."
3. Includes information about all aspects of your future: school, family, relationships, work, spiritual, social, physical, emotional, financial, others.
4. Congruent with your values and life purpose, vision and dreams, and mission.
5. Your commitments are your own, not derived from others.

I am Committed to:

The Success Predictor

Goals

Many of us think that our goals are our dreams. When we asked a young adult what his dreams for his life were, he answered with much confidence, "My dream is to go to Harvard!" But very shortly thereafter, he said with more uncertainty, "I guess that is a goal and not a dream. I guess I really don't know what my dreams are or even how to dream."

Dreams are conceived at higher levels in The Success Predictor, and goals take on more meaning when they are aligned with purpose, mission, vision, and commitments. Goals have a unique importance. Goals are where the "rubber meets the road" or where we need to be accountable for taking action to make our dreams a reality.

Getting into and going to a college, university, or professional school is only a goal, a step along the way toward realizing dreams. The related vision for the young man's particular goal might be "to train with the greatest minds in my field on how to impact society's problems."

One of the defining characteristics of a goal is that it is a statement about what you will do or accomplish and by when—for example, "My goal is to earn acceptance to Harvard by May of this year." Notice the "what," earning acceptance into Harvard, and the "when," by May.

Another example of a goal statement would be "to complete the Boston Marathon next April." The related dream would be "to have greater physical well-being and to experience the transformation from poor health to exhilarating achievement."

Goals bridge your higher purpose, dreams, and commitments to the strategies you will utilize to manifest these. Include information about all aspects of your future: projects you would like to complete, social life, family relationships, physical conditioning, mental well-being, and professional accomplishments, among others.

Your goals should excite you, empower you to act, and be congruent with your dreams; meaning they should be things you *want* to accomplish. President Franklin D. Roosevelt prepared a long list of goals for his life when he was 14 years old, and on this list was becoming President of the United States!

Helpful Hint: Here are some characteristics of effective goal statements:

1. Present tense, e.g., "I will increase my running distance to five miles by my next birthday."
2. Include specific references to your broader vision or dreams for your life.
3. Include information about all of your future goals: school, family, relationships, work, spiritual, social, physical, emotional, financial, others.
4. Congruent with your values and life purpose, and life dreams.
5. Precise and concise; each goal is about one or two sentences in length.

My Goals are:

The Success Predictor

The "how" contextual levels of understanding

Strategies, Plans and Tactics

Using the example of running the Boston Marathon—which is a step along the way toward realizing your dreams of great health and well-being—you need to formulate strategies, plans, and tactics that will help you achieve this goal. Said another way, strategies, plans, and tactics answer the question "how" to achieve your goals.

Consider many strategic alternatives for each of your goals, and decide among them and then pursue. For example, you will need to adopt a new training regimen and more healthy nutrition. These are two strategies—training and nutrition—to achieve the goal and align with your dreams and life purpose.

Completing The Success Predictor is a plan that is an integral part of these strategies, and you will be taking action steps, or tactics, that fulfill the plan.

If you want to get personalized coaching on how to achieve your goals and formulate the strategic alternatives, you may want to enroll in a workshop. You will need to put the time in your schedule, make arrangements for family obligations, and make plans to travel to the workshop location. These tactics will lead to achieving the stated goal.

In this category you will formulate several strategies, as well as the concrete plans and tactics for each strategic alternative.

Helpful Hint: Here are some characteristics of effective strategies, plans, and tactics:

1. Tied directly to specific goals, e.g., "I will enroll into a Personal Well-Being Workshop, map out a route, make family arrangements and then drive to the workshop to give myself personal time to reflect."
2. Include specific references to your goals for your life.
3. Include information about all of your future goals: school, family, relationships, work, spiritual, social, physical, emotional, financial, others.
4. Congruent with your values and life purpose, and life dreams.
5. List each of your goals articulated in the previous category, and then formulate one or two strategic alternatives for each.
6. Plans and tactics address the "how," should be tied directly to each strategic alternative, and be very specific in their descriptions.

My Strategies, Plans, and Tactics for each of my Goals are:

The Success Predictor

The "evidence" contextual level of understanding

Results

Results provide evidence that you are on the right track toward manifesting your purpose, vision, mission, commitments, goals, strategies, and plans. Results serve as your compass for where you want to get to. Results are what occurs after you take action. Results are what you have in your life, and you can check in with yourself to determine if the results you have produced are what you want and whether they align with your dreams and goals.

Results can be intangible, such as feelings of excitement and pride running with others in the Boston Marathon, and tangible, such as crossing the finish line and receiving a medal of completion.

You are producing results constantly in your life, whether tangible or intangible, and you can determine if these are the ones you want, that represent your higher purpose and mission in life, or not.

Sometimes it is helpful begin with the results in mind as a focus, and then determine the other categories from this category of understanding. Ask what results you want to produce in your life in the world, and then work your way back up The Success Predictor categories. These results you want to produce should be closely aligned with those you formulated in your vision statement.

The Results I want to produce are:

Chapter 9

Building Your Support Team

Now that you have completed The Success Predictor, you have the opportunity to put together team members upon whom you can rely to support the new you, your transformed self, and the future you are creating. Support is important—you cannot do this life alone.

What is meant by support?

Support can fall into a number of categories. Often people think that if we are "there" listening to another person's problems, concerns, issues, then we are supporting them. Listening non-judgmentally is a first step, but then you want someone who can offer you guidance on next steps, even if they take you out of your comfort zone. Reflect upon the very recent experience of completing The Success Predictor and determine for yourself, if the other people in your life are just "there" for you, would that help you achieve your desired results?

Support is present when the people in your life are empowering you to transform the quality of your life by keeping you honest with yourself, your life purpose, vision, and commitments. Support is present when you have made big promises in your life to empower yourself, and other people will interact with you based upon your promises.

You either have what you want or all of the reasons why not. Support is when the people in your life help you get what you want, and do not support you in coming up with reasons why not, or reinforcing your reasons why not. (You may have enough of your own.)

If the people in your life do not fit these criteria, then it is time to make some changes in the way people interact with you by making clear requests and communicating with intention. Sometimes, often times, it is appropriate to get an entire new set of people in your life to *really* support what you are up to.

People who share a similar purpose or mission make mutually empowering supporters, and since they may not look or sound like you, be open to making new connections.

Clarify what you are really asking someone to do—whether you are requesting they be a source of ongoing empowerment or help you with one specific task. Some people may prefer another role on your team than your original request, so negotiate what works best for both of you. Some people may decline your request to be on your support team, which is absolutely fine, and their choice. Do not read too much into it, understand they are on their own journey, wish them well, and reach out to another person.

~ REFLECTION ~
Building your support team

Please list in the space provided the people you want on your support team. These are people you want to have supporting you in creating the life you want, one consistent with your purpose, vision, mission, and commitments.

Please describe the role they will play—what you want them to do as members of your team. If you do not have a specific person in mind, write down the role, and then make plans to research, inquire about, and secure the necessary expertise.

It is very often useful to request the support of a "coach," someone who is committed to your transformation, someone who is committed to *you*. We are committed to your transformation.

Support Team

Name   **Role**

1.

2.

3.

4.

5.

6.

And more ...

Chapter 10

Acknowledging Yourself and Others

Bringing The Success Predictor into your life requires celebrating progress. To continue learning just how great you are, acknowledge even the most minute results or accomplishments throughout your daily life.

~ REFLECTION ~
Acknowledging your results

Often, we are not aware we are producing results all of the time, almost on a continuous basis. Take the time to look deeply and list at least 10 results that you produced today:

Results

1.

2.

3.

4.

5.

6.

7.

8.

9.

10.

And more …

Also acknowledge others in your life for what they have done for you thus far. It is truly powerful to experience the depth of joy and happiness and love with those who have meant so much to you.

You have spent time reading this book, actively doing the Reflections, making choices about what you want, and learning about how to create a new self, among others. By reflecting on well-being, the Integrated Self Model, vision techniques, and The Success Predictor, you have been increasing your ability to create the life you want and can envision, based upon your own personal definition of success. You have *directly* participated in the creative, life transformation process.

An essential part of the creative process is acknowledging what has happened (either full success or completing an important step.) By doing so, you suggest to the inner self that you are on the right track. You also give your inner self the additional suggestion that you accomplish what you set out to accomplish.

~ REFLECTION ~
Giving and receiving acknowledgement

For many, giving and receiving acknowledgement takes practice:

- Make a point of fully acknowledging the steps you have taken since reading this book.
- Begin to notice and be open to the acknowledgement you receive in your daily life from others.
- Acknowledge frequently those people in your life who have contributed to you, your development, your success, your happiness.

Expressing your purpose in everyday life

Who among us has gone through life without knowing who we are, or without having a paradigm to guide us in understanding who we are and why we do the things we do? Perhaps if we had known who we were, we could have accessed deeper experiences in our relationships. We could have had more accomplishments academically and better job prospects that more closely mirrored our innate nature and talents.

By gaining a more thorough understanding of our unique potential, we can find a more direct pathway to reaching it, as we navigate this fast-paced contemporary life, characterized by rapid change. During the times in which overwhelming personal and professional crises threaten our mental and physical health, we must find the spiritual, psychological, and emotional resources and methods we need to get through these periods.

This book drew upon research and best practices in a wide variety of human development disciplines where self-knowledge is considered an important protective factor. As we teach numerous attributes of the self in our families, counseling sessions, workshops, and classrooms, people should emerge from their life experiences more able to be well, with a greater understanding of what it means to be healthy—emotionally, physically, intellectually, psychologically, and spiritually. A happy, healthy, flourishing and successful life will stem from well-being and contribute to it, and impact our humanistic concerns.

To paraphrase archetypal psychologist Thomas Moore (1992), the "great malady" of our times is the "loss of soul." And when soul is neglected, it doesn't just go away, it appears "symptomatically as obsessions, addictions, violence, and loss of meaning."

Throughout this book, we discussed models of self, personal transformation, and psychological well-being that are holistic and can be implemented through your everyday life.

We hope and pray you are empowered and better equipped to proactively address your own being level and express your soul.

Revisiting your purpose for new beginnings

Through the months and years ahead, revisit your Success Predictor and the other Reflections to open new possibilities for growth, remind yourself of your evolving purpose, and recognize your accomplishments. Make your purpose a part of your daily life. There is a dynamic relationship between expressing your purpose and continuing to learn about it from your daily experiences. Your purpose will develop as you express, learn, and grow.

Your purpose is at work even through the most difficult times, even when you are frightened, angry, and imperfect. As a human being in the world, you will at some point in time experience doubts, breakdowns on your path, and resistance from other people, and even from your own ego to the new directions you are pursuing. Whether you are feeling accomplished or stuck, happy or sad, reconnect with the possibilities you have imagined, and remind yourself of your purpose to regain focus, energy, and hope.

Being awake to your life purpose and desire to make a difference for others does not mean you need to sacrifice your happiness and fulfillment for others, nor to keep people in your life who are hurtful. Your purpose begins with uplifting *your* life first.

Sometimes it may feel as though you are holding what seem to be two conflicting thoughts or emotions. At those times, use the word "and" to combine the two thoughts to further emphasize to yourself that your purpose and possibilities lead the way. For example, you can be sad at any given moment *and* still be making good choices that help manifest your life purpose. You can have a feeling you have slid backwards *and* still choose positive actions in the present moment. You can be working hard *and* be joyful!

You will begin to gain a deep sense of self-responsibility to uphold your purpose as a part of an interconnected world. When you connect with your purpose, you will call upon your internal resources—self-knowledge, courage, and resilience—and your external resources—information, partnerships and support.

When you recognize new possibilities in your life that are aligned with your purpose, remember in that moment we are proud of you as a partner in making this a better world.

We believe, and deep inside ourselves know, we can help by bringing all of the positive developments and knowledge about well-being into the mainstream of contemporary life for all people. What keeps us motivated is the possibility of actually impacting the human condition, of providing perspectives and approaches that can help people get on track and create pathways to happy, healthy, and flourishing lives. We are blessed to have discovered this for ourselves, and we hope to help others with what we have learned.

If you have been helped in some small way, either personally or professionally, by reading this book or using it in your life, you have honored us. And more importantly, you have honored your self.

A Note to Our Readers

If you have your own examples of how these methods have worked for you, we would be interested in hearing from you. Please email us to share your experiences:
Henry@Brzyckigroup.com
or
Elaine@Brzyckigroup.com.

If you would like to delve deeper into any of the concepts and self attributes presented in this book, please refer to our three previous books listed in the bibliography and here:

The Self in Schooling: How to Create Happy, Healthy, Flourishing People in the 21st Century, ISBN: 0988716100

Student Success in Higher Education: Developing the Whole Person through High-Impact Practices, ISBN: 0988716155

Mental Health for All Toolkit: Teachers, Parents, and Students, ISBN: 0988716186

Bibliography

Achor, S. 2010. *The Happiness Advantage*. New York: Random House.

Bandura, A., Barbaranelli, C., Caprara, G. V., & Pastorelli, C. 2001. "Self-Efficacy Beliefs as Shapers of Children's Aspirations and Career Trajectories." *Child Development* 72(1): 187–206.

Beattie, M. 1987. *Codependent No More*. New York: Harper & Row Publishers.

Borysenko, J. 1987. *Minding the Body, Mending the Mind*. Reading, MA: Addison-Wesley.

Bradshaw, J. 1990. *Homecoming: Reclaiming and Championing Your Inner Child*. New York, NY: Bantam Books.

Brown, F., & LaJambe, C. 2016. *Positive Psychology and Well Being: Applications for Enhanced Living*. San Diego, CA: Cognella.

Brzycki, E. J. & Brzycki, H. G. 2019. *Mental Health for All Toolkit: Teachers, Parents, and Students*. State College, PA: BG Publishing.

Brzycki, E. J. & Brzycki, H. G. 2016. *Student Success in Higher Education: Developing the Whole Person through High-Impact Practices*. State College, PA: BG Publishing.

Brzycki, H. G. 2013. *The Self in Schooling: Theory and Practice: How to Create Happy, Healthy and Flourishing Children in the 21 Century*. State College, PA: BG Publishing.

Brzycki, H. G. 2010. "The Self in Teaching and Learning." In *Educational Psychology Reader: The Art and Science of How People Learn*, edited by G.S. Goodman, pp. 681–700. New York: Peter Lang.

Campbell, J. 1990. *Transformations of Myth through Time*. New York: NY: Harper Row Publishers.

Centers for Disease Control and Prevention. 2011. *Public Health Action Plan to Integrate Mental Health Promotion and Mental Illness Prevention with Chronic*

Bibliography

Disease Prevention, 2011–2015. Atlanta: US Department of Health and Human Services.

Damasio, A. 1994. *Descartes' Error: Emotion, Reason, and the Human Brain*. New York: Penguin.

Dewey, J. 1934. *Art as Experience*. New York, NY: Penguin Books.

Erikson, E. 1980. *Identity and the Life Cycle*. New York: Norton.

Felitti, V. J., & Anda, R. F., 2009. "The Relationship of Adverse Childhood Experiences to Adult Medical Disease, Psychiatric Disorders, and Sexual Behavior: Implications for Healthcare." In *The Hidden Epidemic: The Impact of Early Life Trauma on Health and Disease*, edited by R. Lanius & E. Vermetten. Cambridge: Cambridge University Press. http://www.unnaturalcauses.org/assets/uploads/file/ACE%20Study-Lanius.pdf

Felitti, V. J., Anda, R. F., Nordenberg, D., Williamson, D. F., Spitz, A. M., Edwards, V., Koss, M. P., & Marks, J. S. 1998. "Relationship of Childhood Abuse and Household Dysfunction to Many of the Leading Causes of Death in Adults: The Adverse Childhood Experiences (ACE) Study." *American Journal of Preventive Medicine* 14: 245–58.

Friend, J. H. & Guralnik, D. B. 1953. *Webster's New World Dictionary*. Boston, MA: Houghton Mifflin Harcourt.

Fritz, R. 1984. *The Path of Least Resistance*. Salem, MA: DMA, Inc.

Frost, R. 1949. Happiness Makes Up in Height for What It Lacks in Length, in *The Poetry of Robert Frost*. New York, NY: Henry Holt and Company.

Gabriel García Márquez Quote. (n.d.). *HispanaGlobal.net*. Retrieved April 12, 2021, from *HispanaGlobal.net* website: https://hispanaglobal.net/10-amazing-quotes-from-latino-authors/

Gardner, H. 1983. *Frames of Mind: The Theory of Multiple Intelligences*. New York: Basic Books.

Bibliography

Gilligan, C. 1982. *In a Different Voice: Psychological Theory and Women's Development.* Cambridge, MA: Harvard University Press.

Gilmour, D. & Waters, R. 1979. *Comfortably Numb.* Surrey, England: Pink Floyd Music Publishers Ltd.

Goleman, D. 1995. *Emotional Intelligence: Why It Can Matter More than IQ.* New York: Bantam Books.

Gorman, A. 2021. *The Hill We Climb and other Poems.* New York: Penguin Random House.

Harter, S. 1999. *The Construction of the Self: A Developmental Perspective.* New York: Guilford Press.

Hillman, J. 1996. *The Soul's Code: In Search of Character and Calling.* New York: Random House.

Hillman, J. 1999. *The Force of Character and the Lasting Life.* New York, NY: Random House.

Joyce, J. 1916. *Portrait of the Artist as a Young Man.* New York, NY: Penguin Books.

Jung, C. G. 1970. *The Structure and Dynamics of the Psyche (Collected Works of C.G. Jung, Volume 8).* New York, NY: Bollingen Foundation.

Lopez, S. 2009. *Hope, Academic Success, and the Gallup Student Poll.* Omaha, NE: Gallup.

Marcia, J. E. 1991. "Identity and Self Development." In *Encyclopedia of Adolescence* (vol. 1), edited by R. Lerner, A. Peterson, & J. Brooks-Gunn. New York: Garland.

Marcia, J. E. 2002. "Identity and Psychosocial Development in Adulthood." *Identity: An International Journal of Theory and Research* 2:7-28.142.
Moore, T. 1992. *Care of the Soul: A Guide for Cultivating Depth and Sacredness in Everyday Life.* New York: HarperCollins.

Bibliography

Odum, H. T. 1988. "Self-Organization, Transformity, and Information." *Science* 242: 1132–1139.

Orth, U., Robbins, R. W., & Widaman, K. F. 2012. "Life-Span Development of Self-Esteem and Its Effects on Important Life Outcomes." *Journal of Personality and Social Psychology* 102(6): 1271–88.

Pablo Picasso Quotes. (n.d.). *BrainyQuote.com*. Retrieved April 12, 2021, from *BrainyQuote.com* website: https://www.brainyquote.com/quotes/pablo_picasso_108723

Ryff, C. D., & Keyes, C. L. M. (1995). The structure of psychological well-being revisited. *Journal of Personality and Social Psychology*, 69(4), 719–727.

Seligman, M. E. P., & Csikszentmihalyi, M. 2000. "Positive Psychology: An Introduction." *American Psychologist* 55:5–14.

Shaw, G. B. 1962. *Man and Superman*. New York: Heritage Press.

Shaw, G. B. 1921. *Back to Methuselah*. Biblio Bazaar.

Silverstein, S. 1974. Colors, from *Where the Sidewalk Ends*. Harper Collins.

Smith, W. 2018. "Fault vs Responsibility: Instagram Stories." Retrieved April 12, 2021 from https://www.youtube.com/watch?v=Lm7YEQCckuI.

Swarbrick, M. 2006. "A Wellness Approach." *Psychiatric Rehabilitation Journal* 29(4): 311–14.

Wiesel, E. 1960. *Night*. New York: Hill & Wang.

Williamson, M. 1992. *A Return to Love: Reflections on the Principles of A Course in Miracles*. New York, NY: Harper Collins.

World Health Organization. 2018. *Mental Health: Strengthening our Response*. Accessed https://www.who.int/news-room/fact-sheets/detail/mental-health-strengthening-our-response

About the Authors

Elaine and Henry have generated a body of work to impact the human condition, because they have been called to make the world better. By exploring their life purposes, they have generated possibilities for people to create happy, healthy, and flourishing lives.

For 40 years their work has transformed individual lives, families, K-12 schooling, higher education, and communities, all to create a kinder, safer, and caring world. Their body of work includes:

- Three (3) best-selling books
- Numerous articles and research studies
- Over 50 personal and professional development workshops and courses
- Founding The Brzycki Group & The Center for the Self in Schools

Henry earned his Ph.D. from The Pennsylvania State University, his M.A. from Tufts University, and his B.S. from Babson College. As Dean of the School of Education at American Public University, he transformed teacher and counselor education programs to reflect visionary models of education. Elaine earned an Ed.M. from the Harvard University Graduate School of Education and a B.A. from Wellesley College. She has led cross-functional teams in higher education to develop and deliver educational content on multiple media platforms for student engagement and public awareness initiatives.

Because of Elaine and Henry's large body of work, people are prioritizing mental health and well-being in their own individual lives, families, schools, colleges and universities, and communities.

Elaine and Henry's work has inspired a generation through new policies and best practices in K-16 education, and in mental health and well-being therapeutic and medical settings. Their work as thought leaders helped give birth to and has pioneered best practices in K-12 public school education: social emotional learning (SEL), trauma informed practices, and growth mindset and personalized learning. In colleges and universities their high impact practices have been used in counseling and psychological services (CAPS), academic advising, career counseling, student engagement, and faculty teaching.

Their latest book meets the needs of our times for impactful mental health and well-being techniques. Capturing their counseling expertise and course and program development for individuals, couples, families, and schools, Elaine and Henry have produced a book of methods and resources that will transform your life.

Their work has led to a new societal consciousness about the importance of placing mental health and well-being at the center of creating a good and successful life. Utilized in over 50 countries, their work is making mental health and well-being possible throughout the world.

This book meets the needs of our time, and your own unique needs just in time.

CPSIA information can be obtained
at www.ICGtesting.com
Printed in the USA
LVHW081820110522
718514LV00021B/131